Comments on other *Amazing Stories* from readers & reviewers

*"You might call them the non-fiction response to Harlequin
romances: easy to consume and potentially addictive."*
Robert Martin, *The Chronicle Herald*

*"Tightly written volumes filled with lots of wit and humour
about famous and infamous Canadians."*
Eric Shackleton, *The Globe and Mail*

*"This is popular history as it should be ...
For this price, buy two and give one to a friend."*
Terry Cook, a reader from Ottawa, on **Rebel Women**

*"Stories are rich in description, and
bristle with a clever, stylish realness."*
Mark Weber, *Central Alberta Advisor*, on **Ghost Town Stories II**

*"The resulting book is one readers will want
to share with all the women in their lives."*
Lynn Martel, *Rocky Mountain Outlook*, on **Women Explorers**

"[The books are] *long on plot and character and short
on the sort of technical analysis that can be dreary
for all but the most committed academic."*
Robert Martin, *The Chronicle Herald*

*"A compelling read. Bertin ... has selected only the most intriguing
tales, which she narrates with a wealth of detail."*
Joyce Glasner, *New Brunswick Reader*, on **Strange Events**

*"The heightened sense of drama and intrigue, combined with a
good dose of human interest is what sets* Amazing Stories *apart."*
Pamela Klaffke, *Calgary Herald*

HOLIDAY
MISADVENTURES

AMAZING STORIES®

HOLIDAY MISADVENTURES

Tragedy, Murder, and Mystery

JOYCE GLASNER
JOHANNA BERTIN
ANDREW HIND & MARIA DA SILVA
RICH MOLE

PUBLISHED BY ALTITUDE PUBLISHING CANADA LTD.
1500 Railway Avenue, Canmore, Alberta T1W 1P6
www.altitudepublishing.com
www.amazingstories.ca
1-800-957-6888

Extreme care has been taken to ensure that all information presented in
this book is accurate and up to date. Neither the author nor the
publisher can be held responsible for any errors.

Publisher	Stephen Hutchings
Associate Publisher	Kara Turner
Editor	Lori Burwash
Cover and Layout	Bryan Pezzi

We acknowledge the financial support of the Government
of Canada through the Book Publishing Industry Development
Program (BPIDP) for our publishing activities.

Altitude GreenTree Program
Altitude Publishing will plant twice as many trees as were used
in the manufacturing of this product.

Library and Archives Canada Cataloguing in Publication

Holiday misadventures / Joyce Glasner ... [et al.].

(Amazing stories)
ISBN 1-55439-236-5 (pbk.)

1. Christmas. I. Glasner, Joyce II. Title. III. Series: Amazing
stories (Calgary, Alta.)

GT4985.H65 2008   394.2663   C2006-904748-0

Amazing Stories® is a registered trademark of Altitude Publishing Canada Ltd.

Printed and bound in Canada by Friesens
2 4 6 8 9 7 5 3 1

Contents

Introduction

The true-life accounts featured in this unusual Christmas collection may vary in theme, topic, style, and even region, but they all explore the darker side of the season. Christmas is the one time of the year when most of the country puts aside the demands of everyday life to celebrate with holiday cheer. What happens, though, when life simply won't step aside for Christmas? Amazing Stories® authors Joyce Glasner, Johanna Bertin, Andrew Hind, Maria da Silva, and Rich Mole bring to life the tragic, mysterious, harrowing, chilling, murderous, and inspiring stories of Christmastime gone awry. These tales of struggle, disaster, and adventure remind us to count ourselves lucky if we are able to enjoy a peaceful holiday season and the love of family and friends this Christmas.

Chapter 1
Castaway Christmas
by Joyce Glasner

aptain Henry McArthur was in his cabin nursing a violent attack of rheumatism on the afternoon of December 22, 1881, when his first mate, Charles Carroll, arrived at his door with disturbing news.

At that time, the *Milton*, a 1400-tonne, full-rigged vessel from Nova Scotia, was northbound off the coast of Colombia. Four months earlier, she had set sail for San Francisco from Newcastle, England, carrying 1740 tonnes of coal. Although every precaution had been taken to keep the volatile cargo well ventilated, the equator's sultry temperatures had pushed the coal to the point of combustion. Fire had broken out on the vessel's port side, forward of the mizzenmast.

The alarming news made McArthur forget the crippling

pain that had driven him to his cabin. Grabbing his cap, he hurried out to assess the situation.

A short, powerfully built man with an iron will and a calm, commanding personality, McArthur was a born captain. He rarely rushed into anything without first considering the consequences. As a result, he had survived many harrowing situations. But none had been as dire as this. The fact that his vessel and crew of 19 were in grave danger was bad enough, but to make matters worse, McArthur's wife, Kate, and their two sons, four-year-old Archie and two-year-old Frankie, were also on board.

Before the crew could begin battling the blaze in the cargo hold, they had to clear a path through the coal in order to reach the seat of the fire. The heat and smoke in the hold were intense, making the task all the more difficult. As they shovelled their way through the brittle cargo, sweat streamed down their blackened faces, and deadly smoke and fumes scorched their lungs. All aboard were relieved when they finally reached the fire's source — the heavy canvas hose was hauled into place, and they began dousing the blazing coal. With all available hands fighting the fire, McArthur and Carroll were cautiously optimistic they would soon have it under control.

Once ignited, however, the coal proved impossible to extinguish. By midnight, the fire had spread and the buildup of noxious gas and heat in the hold was deadly. McArthur knew that if he kept the men below any longer, he would be putting their lives at risk.

But he wasn't willing to give up the fight just yet.

After some consideration, it dawned on McArthur that by cutting holes in the deck, they could continue to battle the blaze from above. The order to cut sections out of the deck was quickly carried out, and McArthur and his crew redoubled their firefighting efforts. Those not involved with operating the pump and hose worked the bucket brigade. But it seemed the conflagration was insatiable.

By 2:30 a.m. the situation was critical. All hands had been labouring under extreme duress for at least 12 solid hours. The men were exhausted, and the fire was out of control. The situation was exacerbated by the fact that noxious gases had begun seeping out the hatchways. There was a distinct possibility the vessel could explode at any moment.

Never one to give in easily, McArthur would have kept fighting until the bitter end, but when he glimpsed Kate watching anxiously from across the deck, Frankie in her arms and Archie clinging to her skirts, he realized the fight was over. His vessel was lost. Feeling drained and defeated, he ordered Carroll to have the lifeboats hoisted out and lowered into the Pacific's inky waters.

McArthur was well aware that they could be in the open boats for weeks or even months before being rescued. With this in mind, he had the crew load as much food, water, bedding, and supplies as they could salvage into the lifeboats. While Kate and the crew rounded up provisions, the captain scrambled to retrieve his log, as well as the charts, compass, and sextant from his cabin. Without these vital implements, he would be forced to rely on dead reckoning to stay on course.

Despite his forethought and preparations, McArthur was undoubtedly filled with foreboding as he helped his pregnant wife and two small sons into the boat that night. Frankie was so young — just a baby, really — and Kate was nearly eight months' pregnant. Being an experienced mariner, McArthur would have been painfully aware of the odds against them ever setting foot on land again. The sea is a merciless environment at the best of times. In a small open boat thousands of kilometres from the nearest land, it can be downright treacherous. Perils such as gales, pounding surf, and pirates could bring a tragic end to their voyage at any time. But the greatest threat to their survival would likely be a lack of food and water.

Fortunately, the *Milton* was equipped with three lifeboats, enough to comfortably accommodate all aboard and their supplies. The captain's boat, a roomy, two-masted craft seven metres long by two wide, was the largest of the three. Kate, the two boys, and six of the crew sailed with McArthur. The second boat was commanded by Charles Carroll. With Carroll were six more crew members. The third boat, commanded by the second mate, 18-year-old Edward Anthony, was known as the captain's gig. The smallest of the three boats, the gig was a narrow, one-sailed vessel normally used for transporting passengers to and from the ship when in harbour. With Anthony were the remaining five men.

McArthur saw to it that the supplies from the *Milton* were divided equally among the three boats. In addition to canned meats and vegetables, each boat was granted one smoked ham. Although it wasn't much, the captain estimated that, with careful rationing, they would have enough food and water to last a little over a month.

Although at the time it was unusual for a captain's wife and family to accompany him on his voyages, it wasn't completely unheard of. Faced with the choice of a lonely life ashore or by her husband's side at sea, many captains' wives chose the latter. Being a strong-willed sea captain's daughter, Kate had decided at an early age that if she were to marry a seafarer, she wouldn't sit home alone, waiting for him to return once or twice a year. She married Henry McArthur when she was just 18, and a few days after the wedding, the couple set sail for New Orleans. Her introduction to the seafarer's life was far more dramatic than she'd ever imagined. Shortly after they arrived in port, their ship caught fire and burned to the water-line, leaving the newlyweds homeless and stranded.

In retrospect, that first fire seemed eerily prophetic.

After abandoning the *Milton*, the survivors rowed about a kilometre off, where they remained the rest of the night. The spectacle of the massive vessel being consumed by fire was strangely mesmerizing. The ruddy glow lit up the night sky for kilometres. Clouds of smoke and sparks billowed high above the blazing spars, and the crackling and snapping of flaming timbers echoed across the glassy waters.

At daybreak, McArthur conferred with his first mate. Since abandoning ship, he'd been pondering their situation and charting a course to the nearest land mass. By the captain's estimation, this was Cape San Lucas, California, some 2048 kilometres north of their current position. Between them and Cape San Lucas were the equatorial currents, which could easily drive them hundreds of kilometres off course. Once past the capricious currents, they faced an exhausting struggle against the northeast trade winds.

When they first took to the boats, McArthur was fairly confident they had enough supplies to sustain them on their journey, but after taking these factors into consideration, he worried that the food and provisions they'd salvaged wouldn't be enough. After he discussed the situation with Carroll, the first mate volunteered to go back aboard the ship with another man to scrounge up more supplies.

It wasn't long before the pair returned empty-handed. The heat and smoke aboard the vessel were so intense, Carroll reported, that it was impossible for him to get below to where the provisions were stored. They would just have to make do with what they had.

By the morning of December 24, all that remained of the once stately *Milton* was a blackened, smouldering skeleton. It was time for the little armada to move on. As they set sail, McArthur prayed they would be spotted and picked up by a passing vessel long before reaching Cape San Lucas.

The start to their voyage was anything but propitious.

Strong winds and heavy seas pummelled the boats throughout the first day and night. At daybreak on Christmas morning, McArthur awoke with a start from a troubled sleep. Looking around, he saw only one boat. The other, commanded by his first mate, had disappeared sometime in the night. The captain hurriedly roused his crew and began scanning the horizon for any sign of the missing men. If the vessel had been swamped, McArthur reasoned, surely there would be a trail of debris indicating where they'd gone down. He ordered Edward Anthony to scour the area for survivors and flotsam while he sailed on ahead in search of the missing boat.

The winds had diminished that day, but the seas were still heavy. As they tossed and heaved on the swells, all aboard kept watch for any sign of the others. As the day wore on, tension mounted and the children grew restless. With all the trauma and upheaval of the past few days, Christmas was probably the last thing on Kate's mind. But as Frankie wriggled and squirmed on her lap that day, and Archie asked *again* when they could go "home," meaning back aboard the *Milton*, her holiday plans must surely have come to mind. Luckily Frankie was too young to understand what Christmas was about, but Archie was old enough to know better. No doubt, he had been quizzing Kate constantly about Santa's arrival.

Back home in the village of Maitland, friends and relatives would have been attending church services, exchanging Christmas boxes, and sitting down to extravagant Christmas dinners that took days to prepare. Christmas aboard a cargo vessel at sea was never the same as one back home. However, captain's wives often went to great lengths to make it as traditional as possible. Stockings were hung on the mantle, the cabin was decorated with whatever was available, and Christmas dinner was a special affair that often included a turkey with all the trimmings and, of course, a plum pudding. Preparing such a feast in the ship's galley, particularly in tropical heat, was a challenge, but it was always well worth the effort.

But that evening, as they drifted in the Pacific Ocean, thousands of kilometres from home, Kate dished out only meagre portions of ham, tinned vegetables, and water.

By nightfall, McArthur finally called off the search for the missing men. The loss of Charles Carroll and the others added a mournful tone to what had already been a miserable Christmas. After tucking the boys in that night, Kate sang them hymns and carols until they dropped off to sleep. Afterward, she lay awake listening to the waves rhythmically lapping against the hull, and staring at the vast canopy of stars overhead.

* * *

On December 29, the gig, commanded by Edward Anthony, dropped out of sight. Again, McArthur spent the day scouring the area for any sign of the missing vessel. But none was found. Fearing they were now alone on their journey north, he ordered the sails unfurled and moved on. It was with great relief that he sighted the craft the following day "about six miles to leeward." McArthur quickly overtook the gig and ordered Anthony to "keep his boat well up to the wind, as he was going too far to leeward."

Not trusting the young man to follow his orders, McArthur decided to make some personnel changes in the boats. Anthony was transferred to the captain's boat and Ole Olsen, an experienced seaman and navigator, was put in command of the gig. The next day, however, the weather turned rough. Before long, they lost sight of the gig again. This time, it was gone for good.

By January 4, the survivors were feeling the effects of constantly battling the elements. Their clothing and bedding had been drenched by the towering waves that crashed over the little vessel in rough weather. And in the tropical humidity, it was impossible to get anything dry. It wasn't long before the bedding began to moulder and rot.

Worse, their provisions were already running low. Although strict rationing of the remaining food and water was implemented, the supplies continued to diminish at an alarming rate. McArthur suspected someone in their party was plundering the larder while his back was turned, but he wasn't sure who it was.

Not long afterward, his suspicions were confirmed. One night, Anthony was at the tiller while Captain McArthur slept.

Something moving along the bottom of the boat caught the young man's attention. It was one of the crew "worming his way aft on his stomach." Certain the man was "bent on securing food or causing trouble," Anthony nudged the captain awake.

McArthur had taken to sleeping with a club at his side in the event of such a situation. Grabbing his weapon, the captain strode back and cracked the man over the head, knocking him unconscious. The sailor was then dragged to the bow of the boat and tied up. While securing him, McArthur discovered that the sailor was carrying a large, "vicious looking" dagger.

McArthur confiscated the dagger, but the incident made him realize that the crew could not be trusted. He and his mate were outnumbered. Once the hunger and thirst became too great, who knew what the sailors were capable of? Mutiny was not something McArthur wanted to contend with, particularly with his wife and children aboard.

By the morning of January 16, the castaways were down to less than four litres of water and a few mouldy pieces of the unappetizing, rock-hard biscuit known as hardtack. At that time, McArthur noted in his log, "Our great distress commenced." Starving and exhausted, his men "lost heart and gave up."

Their hopes were briefly revived, however, when they spied a sail on the horizon "about six miles bearing north." McArthur quickly raised his British ensign "union down" to signify distress and changed tack in an attempt to intercept the other vessel.

But fate wasn't on his side. The sails had gone completely slack. With no wind to push them along, they were forced to pick up the oars and row. Weak from hunger and fatigue, the men were all but useless at the oars. To make matters worse, although the wind had dropped, the seas were still rough. Even if the men had been in top physical condition, rowing through the choppy waves would have been a challenge. Since he was certain rescue was at hand, McArthur tried to encourage the men to row faster by giving each of them more than their daily ration of water.

For a brief time, McArthur was certain the other vessel had spotted them and was attempting to come around. Just then, however, a blinding squall blew in, obscuring the vessel from sight. By the time the squall had passed, the vessel had vanished, along with their hopes of rescue.

Two days later, the food was gone and there wasn't a single drop of water left in the casks. McArthur warned the men not to succumb to the temptation of drinking the sea water as it would only dehydrate them further. But he was certain they disregarded his orders and partook of the salt-water whenever his back was turned.

Eventually, the madness that comes from being surrounded by water but not having a drop to drink began to gnaw at the castaways. Their tongues swelled and lips cracked. For Kate, the thirst was unbearable. But worse than her own thirst was the anguish of hearing her children moan and cry for water and having none to give them. As she lay listlessly in the boat hearing the constant swish of the sea all around her, vivid memories of the sensation of cold, clear liquid sliding over the tongue and down the throat haunted her. In her dreams, every drink of water she'd ever taken came back to tantalize her. It seemed so peculiar to be surrounded by water "so blue, and clear, and cool," and yet "be dying of thirst."

The temptation to drink sea water was overwhelming. In an effort to overcome it, Kate began dipping her scarves in the water and wrapping them about her head and throat. This helped alleviate the burning thirst somewhat. But before long, the effect wore off and the thirst returned and "kept raging worse and worse."

The survivors desperately prayed for rain, but to no avail. Each day, the sun beat down upon them mercilessly, bleaching their hair white and burning their skin black. Occasionally they spied rain clouds off in the distance, but none came their way.

It soon became obvious that no one would survive the ordeal unless they got drinkable water. Unable to sit back and watch his wife and children die of thirst, McArthur came up with the notion of creating a condenser. Using a couple of empty tins and some marlin lashings, he devised a contraption that would produce the drinkable water they all so desperately needed.

In order to make the condenser work, however, fire was

required. Being in a small boat, surrounded by nothing but water, this posed a problem. First, he needed something to build the fire in. More importantly, he needed something to burn. The solution, McArthur discovered, was the tin-covered lid of Kate's steamer trunk. So the trunk lid was turned into a fire pit. Fuel was scavenged from the only available source — the boat itself. McArthur began shaving slivers of wood from the oars, seats, and ribs of the vessel to feed the fire.

The condenser was a godsend, producing about half a litre of water from the vapours in the air every 24 hours. The parched, hollow-eyed survivors huddled around the miraculous invention, counting each drop as it landed in the tin. Once the can was full, the precious water was doled out one sip at a time.

Another blessing came their way on January 28, when a fish suddenly leaped from the water, arched overhead, and landed at their feet with a smack. The fish was quickly gutted and the fire stoked. Although there was only a mouthful of flesh for each, to the starving survivors it seemed like a feast.

Being in her final trimester of pregnancy, Kate should have been eating enough for two. But throughout the ordeal, she ate and drank barely enough to sustain herself, dividing the lion's share of her rations between her two sons in the hope it would keep them alive.

But on February 2, a little over a month after they'd abandoned ship, Frankie died in his mother's arms. The death of her youngest son was too much for Kate to bear. For the first time since setting out, she fell apart. When Henry tried to take Frankie's body from her, she clutched it to her chest and refused to give it up. She simply couldn't stand the thought of the little body being dumped into the ocean, where it was certain to be consumed by sharks.

In an effort to placate her, McArthur swore he wouldn't bury the child at sea. When she finally handed Frankie's body over, he tenderly wrapped it in a tattered piece of canvas and placed it in a tin box. He vowed to bury their child in consecrated ground as soon as they reached land.

Three days after Frankie's death, one of the men also succumbed. The next day, another died. McArthur gravely preformed the burial services and recorded the deaths in his log. By that time, the remaining survivors were little more than skin and bones. The prospect of any of them surviving was beginning to look grim.

It seemed miraculous then, when that very afternoon they sighted land. St. Roques Island was nothing more than a barren rock jutting out of the sea. But to the survivors, it represented salvation. McArthur attempted to make land, but the surf was furiously battering against the steep, rocky shore. It would be suicidal to get too close. He decided to move a safe distance from the island for the night and attempt a landing again the next morning.

Just as he began to come about, McArthur spotted a sail off in the distance. At first he thought his bleary, bloodshot eyes must be playing tricks on him. He rubbed his eyes and raised his telescope for another look. Sure enough, there was a schooner about eight kilometres to the east. He desperately tried to rouse his emaciated crew to help row, but they were too weak to move. Determined not to let what might be their final chance at rescue slip away, McArthur picked up the oars himself and began rowing.

The seas were rough, and the boat bucked and lurched heavily against the waves. In McArthur's weakened condition, it was a struggle to keep going. But he knew that if they weren't rescued that night, he'd be performing more burials the next day.

When the vessel suddenly disappeared from sight, McArthur felt utterly defeated. He lowered his sail and collapsed. About two hours later, however, he caught sight of her again. And again he pushed himself to the limit to reach the vessel. By then darkness was closing in. Hoping to catch the schooner's attention, McArthur began hollering. He shouted until he was hoarse. But the schooner gave no indication of having noticed him. It wasn't until he came within a boat's length of the vessel that they finally acknowledged him.

The vessel, it turned out, was a Mexican schooner. "Lost my ship, the *Milton*, by fire on the equator," McArthur croaked. "And have been 46 days in the boat." Since his voice was all but gone, and he was several metres from those aboard the ship, he couldn't be sure they'd heard, or understood, him. After several minutes, though, the Mexicans cast down a line. For a brief moment it seemed rescue was finally within his grasp.

McArthur's hopes were dashed, however, when no sooner had he latched on to the line than it was abruptly cut, and the schooner's guns trained on him. Although piracy wasn't the threat it had once been, in remote locales such as this, vessels were still vulnerable to attack by cutthroats roaming the seas in search of plunder. Clearly the Mexican captain feared McArthur was one of these buccaneers.

Fortunately, shortly after cutting the line, the Mexican captain had a change of heart. He ordered a skiff lowered into the water. Soon, two men rowed alongside the castaways. When the Mexicans got a look at the skeletal, weather-beaten figures in the boat, they understood what had happened. Kate and young Archie were taken aboard the skiff and rowed over to the schooner first. For McArthur, it seemed like an eternity before the men returned and latched on to his boat.

Once all the survivors had been lifted aboard the *Thor*, they were attended to immediately. For the next few days, Captain Christobal Sosa and the crew of the *Thor* generously shared what little food and water they had with the castaways. "They treated me and my poor starving crew with the greatest kindness and consideration," McArthur reported. However, they barely had enough supplies to sustain themselves. So when an American steamer happened along a few days later, the castaways parted company with their rescuers and transferred over to the steamer.

The *Newburn,* commanded by Captain Thomas Huntington, was heading for a Mexican port on the Gulf of California. Huntington offered to deliver McArthur and his party to San Francisco after completing his business. He also had some very welcome news for the Nova Scotians. It turned out the gig commanded by Ole Olsen had been picked up on January 15 and taken to San Francisco. All aboard Olsen's boat had survived and were anxiously awaiting word of the fate of McArthur and the others.

Although the castaways were now being showered with the best of care, the punishing ordeal had left them weak and ill. Their lives were still hanging in the balance. Shortly after boarding the *Newburn,* one man, who had been hovering near death since the rescue, succumbed.

When Kate McArthur was helped aboard the *Newburn,* her appearance was shocking. Her long, blonde hair hung in tangles around her shoulders. Her cheeks were sunken, and her lips white and cracked. Her grey eyes appeared hauntingly pale in contrast to her deeply tanned skin. Her ragged dress sagged on her emaciated frame. Anyone seeing her would have found it difficult to believe she was nine months' pregnant.

Ten days after their rescue, the *Newburn* was making her way into Guaymas Harbor when Kate went into labour. Although her strength was slowly returning, she was still extremely weak and frail. Too frail, McArthur feared, to survive childbirth.

Castaway Christmas

While McArthur and Archie anxiously paced the deck, several female passengers tended to Kate. The delivery was long and difficult. After many tense hours, McArthur was relieved to finally be summoned to Kate's cabin. Newburn Huntington McArthur weighed only three pounds at birth, but he was strong and healthy. Although Henry McArthur would never get over the loss of his youngest son, Charles Carroll, and the others, the sight of Kate cradling their newborn son in her arms made him feel that he'd been blessed. Providence, he was certain, had watched over them throughout their long, harrowing journey and, in the end, delivered them to this safe harbour.

Bibliography

Glasner, Joyce. *Christmas in Atlantic Canada: Heartwarming Legends, Tales, and Traditions.* Canmore: Altitude Publishing, 2004.

MacMechan, Archibald. *Sagas of the Sea.* Toronto: JM Dent & Sons Ltd., 1923.

"The Burning of the *Milton*." (From *San Francisco Chronicle*) *Nova Scotian*, February 11, 1882.

"The Loss of the *Milton*." (From *San Francisco Chronicle*) *Nova Scotian*, March 25, 1882.

Chapter 2
The Kissing Bough
by Johanna Bertin

Amelia Copeland* held James and Thomas close, shielding her young sons from contact with the dock workers. Portsmouth Harbour in 1799 was teeming with people: sailors and soldiers disembarked from docked vessels and countless others — Amelia included — prepared to embark. There was excitement in the air, shouts in many languages, and a particular coarseness of speech that bothered this sensitive woman but seemed to delight her two sons.

Britain was at war with France, but it wasn't violence that Amelia feared. It was the Moroccan flu, said to have killed 274,000 people in the city of Fez alone. Her husband, Dr. Andrew Copeland, physician to the Duke of Kent, had told her of the latest reports of death in that far-off city.

Amelia knew that flu spread rapidly, and Morocco was but a sea voyage from Portsmouth, England. Anxious to reach the relative isolation of their cabin, she hurried James and Thomas aboard the *Frances*.

The *Frances* was meant to have sailed for Halifax on September 6, 1799, but here it was October 25 and they had not yet left, delayed by the embargo on shipping. Amelia knew that this voyage would be far different from the one a year ago that had brought them to England from Halifax. That time, she and her family had sailed with Prince Edward, Duke of Kent, on HMS *Topaz*. Sailing with Edward had given them luxuries they would not have on this voyage. Meals had been sumptuous, served on the finest porcelain. She and her husband had shared a cabin that was airy and light, and there had been a separate one for the maid and the children. But the brig *Frances* was a transport ship built to carry the maximum number of troops, with little attention to their comfort. The cabins were austere and the meals planned to fill the stomach, not satisfy the palate. Amelia wished once again that Andrew hadn't been quite so determined to accompany the shipment of the duke's possessions.

In May, the duke had been appointed commander in chief of all of British North America, and he intended to live in a far grander style than before. He had asked Andrew to supervise the preparations and shipment of his personal belongings, and Andrew had been busy for weeks. Choosing housewares for a duke hardly seemed a job for a doctor, but

Amelia's husband had accepted it with grace, pleased with the trust in him it displayed. Even now he was late, having been called back to make a decision regarding the fitness of one of the horses to travel.

Amelia and the boys had been assigned the first lieutenant's cabin. Though small, it had light and air and access to the stern weather deck, where they would be allowed to walk once they cleared harbour. Amelia would have settled for almost any accommodation: she just wanted to leave the crisis of flu and famine in England, and focus instead on preparations for the upcoming Christmas and New Year festivities in Halifax.

Thomas tugged at Amelia's sleeve. He had seen the soldiers come aboard, men of the 7th Fusiliers and the 16th Light Dragoons. The soldiers were to escort the duke's belongings, and Thomas and his older brother had become very familiar with several of the regiment.

"Can we go on deck? Please? I want to see if Captain Stirling has come aboard." Captain Stirling was a favourite of Thomas's, full of stories of the regiment that he acted out with all the appropriate sound effects.

James was more reserved among the officers, preferring to spend time with his father, assisting him in the surgery. He wanted to be a doctor himself — a ship's surgeon — and was eager to tour the sick bay below deck.

Thomas tugged at his mother's sleeve again.

"The horses are coming. Can we please go on deck?"

Thomas wanted to be out where the action was, not stuck in a cabin peering around the door. Amelia was tempted. She watched the horses approaching the gangplank, skittish and fretful. There were a team of four Cleveland bays, four chestnuts, two greys, and two brown horses so rich in colour they appeared black. She couldn't imagine a carriage navigating the potholes of Halifax, but the horses were splendid. However, as tempted as she was, and as eager as Thomas was, Amelia knew that the deck would be too dangerous when they readied the horses for the sling that would lower them into the hold.

Instead, she distracted the boys, showing them the special treasures she had packed into her trunk. Nestled on top of her clothing were real holly and a strange object made of two wooden hoops, one fitted through the other. Each hoop was wrapped in evergreen, and in the centre of the hoops were a rosy apple and a sprig of mistletoe. She told the boys it was called a kissing bough and she was taking it home to hang in their foyer for the 12 days of Christmas. They had nothing like it at the market in Halifax.

By noon, the last trunk was stowed and the chickens, goats, and pigs in their pens near the bow. Finally, Amelia spied Andrew coming up the gangplank. James immediately left the cabin and attached himself to his father, certain he would be able to explore more of the ship in his company. But disappointingly, Andrew directed him to stay close to Amelia until the ship cleared harbour. The *Frances,* a two-masted, square-rigged brig, was a manoeuvrable ship and an excellent sailor, but leaving port was fraught with danger of collision with other ships. There would be plenty of opportunity to walk on deck over the next month.

The *Frances* eased out of port and then stood astern while the *America* and HMS *Bonetta* readied to follow. She would not be alone on this trip. Being a transport, she had only 14 guns, little enough against the far superior French warships of Napoleon's navy. The convoy would provide protection — though few people knew the value of the cargo, they could hardly have missed the two carriages with the royal crest. The quality and beauty of the horses, to say nothing of their number, would indicate that the ship carried treasure of immense value. What few but Dr. Copeland and the soldiers knew was that among those supplies were 11,000 pounds sterling of new weaponry and the most current maps and charts — an invaluable prize for any French warship.

At dusk, Amelia chose to eat with her boys in their cabin rather than in the mess with the officers. They entertained themselves thinking of the many changes that would have taken place in their absence: additions to the duke's estate, known as Prince's Lodge; new plays at the theatre; perhaps a new store on Barrington Street. There was so much to look forward to.

* * *

The convoy made good speed and, as no French warships were sighted, James and Thomas were allowed far more freedom on the ship than would normally be the case. James assisted his father in the surgery, and Thomas spent his days with the officers. He was beaming with pride when he announced to his mother that he now knew how to load a cannon. Amelia, free from household responsibilities and sure of her sons' safety, luxuriated in reading the novels she had brought from London.

All that freedom changed when the storms came. They were of such ferocity that the ship seemed to be on end at times. The men high in the rigging had to fasten themselves to the mast because waves swept so high that a man less than four metres up had his boots full of water. Amelia and the boys had been forced to move to a cabin in the lower deck. Their berth on the weather deck was no longer safe, for the sea was so high, it washed over the deck and slammed against the cabin door.

The *Frances* seemed to weather the waves better than the *America* or HMS *Bonetta*. Late one day, Andrew told Amelia that the *America* was no longer with them. The last signal they had received from the missing ship told of damage to her mast, and the captain had lowered her sails in the hope of repairing it before it snapped. But the *America* was also leaking badly, and though she had her pumps working full-time, the captain intended to return to Portsmouth.

Then they ran into snow, heavy snow that swirled about the two ships and prevented them from seeing 30 metres ahead. The seas rose and Amelia and the boys were confined to their cabin, lest they be thrown about the ship or injured by gear come loose from its tether. Every half hour they heard the ship's cannon signal her location, then waited for a response from HMS *Bonetta*. But one morning, the response never came. The *Frances* was now truly alone.

After they suffered through two more days of snow, the weather cleared, and Amelia and the boys had their first hot meal in over a week — the Brodie stove had been put out during the rough seas for fear of fire in the event it tipped. The smell of wood smoke cheered Amelia.

"It smells like home," said Thomas, reflecting her thoughts. Indeed it did. That odd mixture of wood smoke and salt-tinged air peculiar to seaport towns in winter.

"And soon, we shall *be* home," said Amelia. "What do you want to do first, James?"

"I want sweets from the shop on Barrington Street!" piped up Thomas.

"And you, James?" repeated Amelia.

"I want to explore the grounds at Prince's Lodge."

The duke's estate was a fabulous place for children, full of wonders. Edward had had his regiments enlarge the lake and shape it into a heart as a reflection of his love for his companion, Madame Julie Thérèse-Bernardine Montgenet. The gardener had told James that if the boy could fly, he would see that the trails throughout the property had been cut to spell "Julie."

"Do you think Madame will have new sweets at Christmas?" asked Thomas, firmly sticking to topic.

"I am certain," said Amelia, yearning terribly for the safety and security of Halifax and the people they loved.

"Will there be a pantomime like there was in London?" Thomas asked, moving on to a new subject.

"I don't know," replied Amelia. "But we will have the theatre. Though we won't arrive in time for the duke's birthday celebrations, we will certainly arrive home in time for the Christmas balls and theatre and for the New Year's Eve celebration."

But in her heart, Amelia was no longer certain of that. They had lost so much time in the storms and been blown off course — she was no longer even sure where they were.

Amelia was tired of the endless days at sea, frightened at how long it was taking to return home. The expected 27-day crossing was well into its 57th day. They had sailed right through the month of November and it was now December 21. She wasn't the only one feeling the effects. Even the horses were suffering as a result of the long voyage. They little resembled those skittish, beautiful animals that had been loaded onto the ship, but were instead quiet and thin, all suffering from shipping fever. Halifax seemed more and more distant, although logically Amelia knew they must be getting closer. Still, logic did little to quiet her mounting anxiety.

Amelia wanted to walk on pine needles rather than on a deck awash with water. She wanted to sleep in her own bed, not in a cot made to serve as a coffin if necessary. So homesick was she for friends and home that she went to her trunk, lifted the lid, and took out the kissing bough. It looked different now, less cheery. The once rosy apple was brown and shrivelled, the evergreen dry and brittle. Only the sprig of mistletoe and its berries held their original lustre. But she hung it from the centre beam in her cabin and called the boys, giving each a noisy kiss when they entered the berth.

The voyage had not seemed to tire the boys as it had her. They both looked tanned and fit. James had taken on the quiet calm and deportment of his father. Thomas, as boisterous as ever, reported that they would pass by Sable Island tomorrow, and then would have only a day's sailing before reaching Halifax. He was excited, full of tales of the island's reputation. Master Ledmen had told him that the island was called the "Graveyard of the Atlantic." Thomas continued, doing his best to sound just like Master Ledmen: "It's said that there are 200 ships that have wrecked on its shores, that the sand is full of skeletons of the men who drowned there. It's like she's a magnet that pulls ships in … even when you think you've passed her, you dare not relax, for she's tricky, Sable is." What he didn't tell his mother was that if they didn't want to add themselves to that pile of skeletons, they had to make sure Sable stayed to the south of them — far off in the distance.

The next morning, Amelia woke to a beautiful sunrise,

and all her fears of the day before seemed foolish. The wind was calm and Amelia and the boys were able to walk on deck. She felt such relief knowing that they were expected to reach Halifax tomorrow. The trip that had seemed endless would be over. But such weather, a welcome relief to Amelia, spelled only danger. The master of the *Frances,* like so many before him, and many after him, had been lulled by the ocean's calm surface and not felt the inexorable pull of the currents. Far from passing well north of Sable Island as he had planned, they were instead to the southeast — he could actually see sand dunes in the distance.

Amelia didn't understand the danger, thinking they were still miles from the island, but Ledmen knew better. He knew that sand bars extended underwater for about 48 kilometres at the eastern end of Sable Island and that he was lying close off her treacherous northeast bar. As many a time as the *Frances* tried to pull away from Sable, the ship found herself unable to break the island's grasp. There was insufficient wind to fill the sails, and the ship could only hold her own against the current and the surf, could make no headway out to sea.

All that day, Ledmen persevered. He checked the waters and the wind, looking for any change in current or tide — looking for an opening that would free his ship from the island's hold. Amelia felt the heightened tension aboard the *Frances,* heard the change in tone of commands as Ledmen grew more and more worried. She had seen Captain Stirling at the rail, searching the beach through the telescope. She knew that he had seen two men, roughly dressed and unkempt. Rather than being reassured by the chance of rescue that this seemed to hold, he had been alarmed. Amelia was not aware of the reports of wreckers, men who waited on Sable to prey upon victims of shipwrecks. But Stirling knew there would be no help coming from them.

At sunset, the wind picked up, giving those on board renewed hope that the *Frances* would be able to pull away from the island. But as the wind gathered in strength so that it now blew in gusts, it carried with it the scent of blossoms. The fragrance was unfamiliar to Amelia, but readily recognized by Ledmen. Gardenia. Delicate as it was, the scent brought only fear to him. For the wind, which blew with more and more strength, came not from the northwest, as they needed, but from the southeast, a terminal wind for the *Frances.*

Sable Island had come under the assault of a southeast gale that assailed the island with a force generated by the wind's unimpeded travel from its source in the tropics. There was no land mass to absorb the winds, no islands to divert its path, only open ocean for thousands of kilometres. The scent, picked up by the wind at its source, travelled up the coast and slammed against the island. Driven before the onshore wind, carried forward by the waves, and buffeted by the breakers, the *Frances* was being driven closer to the shore.

Andrew took Amelia and their sons on deck from the relative shelter below. Up there, the noise was deafening. The wind tore at the sails, and they loosened and ripped, snapping like cracks of thunder. Water, heavy with sand, washed over them, sweeping everything in its path into the sea. The ship creaked and groaned as if in pain.

The crew struggled to free a pinnace, though it was already far too late to lower it into the water and make for the island. The time had long passed for that escape, for even if they managed to get it onto the water, there was no longer any chance that they would survive being lowered into it, let alone make it to shore. Then even that fiction was gone, as — with a crack like a gunshot — the mast snapped and fell among the pinnaces lashed on deck, shattering them.

The ship rammed into Sable's submerged bar. That is where the waves break from the bottom, and the *Frances*, seaworthy vessel though she was, was no match for the turbulence and was tossed about as if she were a rowboat, not a 280-tonne transport.

Amelia lost her footing, was grabbed by Andrew, and righted herself. She saw Thomas, his face pale but brave, held by Captain Stirling, and James ... Where was James? Frantic, she looked around and caught sight of him, his arms wrapped around the rail.

The ship groaned as she was torn apart, her planks shrieked as they were ripped from the ship's ribbing. And then, as the ship lurched, her rudder jammed into the sand and unshipped with such force that men hanging on to it for security were hurled overboard.

Holiday Misadventures

The sound of destruction was everywhere, so that the tearing sob that arose from Amelia's throat as she saw Thomas and Captain Stirling slip into the sea had no sound. She felt a tug at her clothing as Andrew left her side to try to grasp James as he swept past, his hold on the railing insufficient to fight the water's force. Then they, too, were gone, and Amelia let herself go, carried on a wave that lifted her over the shattered rail. But her skirt caught in the decking and she hung suspended over the sea until finally, with the next wave, the fabric ripped and she rode the water in until it tumbled and battered her, rolled her over and over, bruising her against the sand and the surf.

* * *

On the shore the next morning, Ziba Hunt and Coleman Crowell had not yet risen. The day before, they had watched as the brig tried to draw away from the shore, but they had had to take shelter themselves. They were holed up in a shack, one they had used many a night since they had been left stranded on Sable Island. They were to have been picked up in September, but storms had prevented their sealing captain from mooring, and they had been left on the island to fend for themselves until spring would bring their captain back.

They knew better than to venture out when the winds were so fierce. A blow like that swept up the sand so that it filled your ears and eyes until the only way you could clear the grit was to lean over a smoking fire and let the tears wash it out. It hurt, the smoke did, but not as bad as the grains of sand.

The two men had barely made it to the hut, clinging to each other — their combined weight making it less likely they would blow into the ocean. Even so, the wind picked them up and hurled them along the beach until they found the hut and, getting within its shelter, leaned against the door until it latched shut. They had listened to the wind the night before, felt the force of its fury as the shack shuddered and shook until it seemed as if the island itself was tumbled about. At some point they had fallen asleep, but now they awoke. It was silent, but they did not know how close they were to dawn, for the fog hindered their sight. They remained in the shack until the sound of gulls told them it was day, told them there was wreckage on the beach. The gulls were excited and raucous, made the same calls they made when a whale beached. It was a scavenging call, and Ziba and Coleman heeded it.

They were not bad men, Ziba and Coleman, but sealers placed upon the island to hunt the harp and hooded seals that kitted there. They were accustomed to death, had been the cause of death for hundreds of seals. And they were accustomed to seeing horses on Sable Island. At first they thought that by some mischance, some of the Sable horses had got trapped on the northeast bar in the gale and been swept out to sea and drowned, then washed ashore. But these horses were like no Sable horse. There were two greys

— neither man had ever seen a grey horse on Sable — and, wonder of wonders, they were shod.

Ziba knew then that they had come off the boat, and that if the horses were here, the boat had been torn apart. There were trunks, too, with writing on the sides, but as neither Ziba nor Coleman could read, the words were of no consequence and they had no knowledge that the items belonged to the heir to the throne of England. They had to satisfy themselves with peering inside. They found red wool uniforms in one, a hat in a second, and vials of medicine in a third. It appeared to be a military ship of some sort. Perhaps there would be items they could sell.

There were no bodies on the sand, but Ziba was not surprised. The waters of Sable did not always give up their dead so easily. Sometimes, a body drowned on the south beach would circle the island in the currents and be drawn up onto the north beach.

Farther along the shore they spied a barrel. It was full of biscuits, a welcome relief to their diet of seal and fish. Then a barrel of rum and another of beer. A sea chest was floating in, tossed up on the sand and then dragged back by the pull of a wave. They waded out and pulled it up. On top of dresses of silk there lay a curious contraption — two wooden hoops made to fit into each other, covered in evergreen and white berries. Ziba had never seen anything like it. Deciding it had little value, he tossed it into the waves, content with the trunk and clothing.

They turned back toward the shack. There was no need to hurry to collect items — the sea would continue to bring up treasures over that day and the next. Sometimes it was days later that things appeared. Already there were new things they hadn't seen when they passed in the other direction — a goat and pig, both drowned, and the pieces from several pinnaces.

It was then that Ziba saw the body. For all his comfort with the harvesting of seals, he was shaken. He had never seen the drowned corpse of a woman. He walked reverently to her, knew she was dead by the black bruising on her skin. She looked as if she had been beaten in a fight, but he knew the waves and sand had done that to her, had torn the skin off her cheek. Even then, he could see that her features were delicate, that her clothing was of a quality seen on ladies of wealth. She was not a servant girl, that was for certain.

Ziba and Coleman knew they should bury her. It was only decent, and they needed to do it before the gulls found her, tore strips off her damaged face, plucked out her still-open eyes, such a startling blue. Only her hair had saved them. It had come loose from its braid, lain across her face so that its chestnut tresses covered the eyes, hiding them from the gulls. Ziba found himself uncommonly bashful as he put his hands under her shoulders and lifted her while Coleman wrapped her skirts as best he could around her legs and placed his hands around her ankles. They were silent as they carried her up into the dunes, above the water line of high tide and storm.

Ziba and Coleman stopped of accord beside a hollow. They placed her in it and straightened her clothing. Ziba knelt down to close her eyes. He couldn't bear the thought of sand in those eyes, the colour of the sky over Sable on a winter's day. He crossed her hands over her breast the way he had seen it done when his brother died. And he saw the ring, an intricate twisted metal that he presumed was gold. It seemed a shame to bury it with her — she wouldn't need it where she was going. But her hand was swollen, and the ring stuck fast. Ziba spread sand over her, although he knew that even if he left her uncovered, Sable's winds would bury her. Such a shame, it being almost Christmas, he thought.

* * *

In Halifax, the duke and Julie prepared for the Christmas festivities. Julie knew that Edward was worried about his shipment. It should have arrived long ago. By the strangest turn of fate, he had lost six shipments over the past nine years — five to French privateers or navy ships. The sixth had gone through the ice on Lac Champlain when he had been transferred to Halifax from Quebec. He could not — would not — believe that a seventh could be lost. It would be the financial ruin of him. Besides, he missed young Dr. Copeland, and Julie, usually a cheerful and loving companion, seemed jumpy as of late, worried about the boys. She was devoted to them, and to Amelia, who was one of the few women she had befriended in this city so taken aback by her unmarried liaison with the duke.

On Christmas Day, much of Halifax attended church services, and in the evening, the gentry and officers gathered at Prince's Lodge for the Christmas banquet. When they were all seated, the butler entered, carrying a silver platter on which was the most enormous pig's head, decorated with rosemary, a lemon stuffed in its mouth. Two servants walked beside the butler, carrying huge tapers as if to light his way to the head of the table, and a harpist accompanied his passage. And then were served the dishes of the feast. First came onion soup, then venison and game and fowl — turkey and goose. Then heaping plates of root vegetables. Finally, the feast ended with plum pudding and mincemeat pie and toasts made over sherry and port. Fully sated, the guests danced as the music played and the candlelight enhanced their splendid gowns. It was all brightness and warmth and merriment.

* * *

On Sable that night, the fog swirled around the rats, the only survivors of the wreck, as they clambered over the animal carcasses, bloated with the gas of decomposition. The rats had floated in on trunks or clung to the mast and spars, and now they feasted, as they had not had a chance to do on the ship. Ziba had gone down to the beach to see what else had come in but, discouraged and sickened by the rats, had returned to the shack. He felt as if the cold of the fog was entering into his bones.

He and Coleman ate their supper of biscuits and seal meat and, thinking it must be Christmas, they allowed themselves a swig of rum. And another. They talked about the wreck and wondered about the family of the lady they had found washed up on the sand. Ziba was sure he had seen her on the beach earlier in the day. She had been walking back and forth, searching for something or someone. Though reason told him that it could not be her, that he and Coleman had buried her, he refused to go down to the water unless Coleman went with him.

* * *

On January 1, 1800, the townspeople of Halifax celebrated their new year and the fact that they had survived to see it in. But Edward could not enjoy the celebration, and it was with relief that he saw the decorations come down on January 6. He knew now that his shipment was lost.

In April, news of the *Frances* finally came. Well, not quite news, but one of the maids said that, in a house in town, she had seen a quilt made in the finest red wool, which matched exactly the colour of the regimental uniforms of the Fusiliers. Then a soldier reported to Edward that he had seen a man, not military, wearing an officer's coat on Barrington Street. Another had seen a printer wearing a soldier's linen shirt, distinctively that of the Fusiliers. There was no doubt they were from the *Frances*, but was there not now some hope that more might have been salvaged — that perhaps there were survivors?

In May, Lieutenant Governor Sir John Wentworth sent Lieutenant Scrambler of HM cutter *Trepassey* to investigate. Scrambler reached Sable Island on May 13, but found no one, alive or dead. But he did see a schooner anchored at the northeast spit. He tried to approach her, but the current prevented him from getting within hailing distance. Then, at 4 p.m., he saw the schooner under sail and set a course that transected her path. Scrambler could read her name now — the *Dolphin*, a fishing schooner from Barrington. He suspected she had a cargo of fish, sealskins, and sea oil. But he was looking for other items, and he found them.

On board were several water- and salt-damaged trunks. One was clearly marked "HRH Prince Edward, No. 2." Another belonged to Captain Stirling of the 7th Regiment of Foot. Both were empty, but a third trunk contained two great-coats, the livery worn by the servants of His Royal Highness. Scrambler asked the *Dolphin*'s captain, Reynolds, where he had found them.

Reynolds said that two of his sealers had wintered on the island and had seen the vessel close to the northeast bar, but had been unable to help because of the storm. These trunks were the only items salvaged from the ship. Scrambler saw no reason to doubt him. He had heard tales of Sable Island, of how entire ships disappeared in a storm with no trace.

Scrambler wrote his report, and had his pilot deliver it and the retrieved items to Governor Wentworth. When he did so, the pilot added his own news, for he had spoken directly with the sealers. His input supported Scrambler's report but included some additional information.

The sealers said that the captain had lied about there being no cargo — they saw it washed up on shore along with the drowned carcasses of 12 shod horses, 2 sheep, 2 cows, a bull, a goat, and a pig. There had been barrels of biscuits, several cases of liquor, and parts of several pinnaces.

Wentworth was deeply concerned. Had the pilot asked about survivors? There were none, but there had been one corpse, that of a woman. She had a ring on her finger, the sealers had told him, but, not being able to get it off, they had buried it with her.

Wentworth found this last bit of news particularly disturbing. He was too much the military man to believe that poor sealers would leave a ring on the finger of a dead woman. They were accustomed to butchering animals — would they not just cut off her finger to get an obviously valuable ring? But he had no way of knowing, and although Reynolds was prosecuted for not reporting salvaged goods, Ziba Hunt and Coleman Crowell did not appear to testify. It seemed that nothing more could be done.

The Kissing Bough

In May 1803, Captain Torrens of the 29th Regiment sailed to Sable Island on the gun brig *Harriet* and, like others, wrecked there. Torrens spent four months on Sable before being taken off, and, during his stay, he sought shelter from a storm in the very hut that Ziba and Coleman had used.

The first time Torrens entered the hut, he found a woman seated beside a lit fire, though he had seen no smoke when he approached. She appeared to have come straight from the sea, her clothing clinging to her, her hair dank and flat. But it was the eyes that held him — the clearest blue eyes, full of anguish.

Taking off his uniform coat, Torrens offered it to the lady. At his movement, she held up her hand as if to ward him off, and he saw that it was bloody, that her ring finger was cut off. He looked in his trouser pocket for a handkerchief to bind the wound, but when he looked up, she was gone.

Torrens ran outside but could not see her. His own experience still fresh in his memory, Torrens knew she would die of hypothermia unless he could get her warm and dry. He needed to find her, but first he would get his coat.

He stepped back into the hut, and there she was, seated beside the fire again. Recognizing her then as Amelia Copeland, Torrens knew she must be a ghost, for no woman could survive three years at Sable Island dressed as she was. He had met Mrs. Copeland at a regimental dinner, had known her husband quite well, and had mourned the loss of the family three years before.

"What has happened to your finger, Madame?" he asked. Surely it was as important to maintain courtesy with a ghost as with a living woman.

"He cut off my finger," she replied. "Cut it off for my ring."

Was this why she could find no peace? But this woman had lost a husband and her children. Would a ring be of much importance to her?

She seemed to understand the question, though he had not spoken. "It is because they butchered me to steal it from me," she said calmly. "My family was lost by accident, but the theft was evil, and because of that I cannot rest. If you could but return it to me, I would be at peace."

"How is it that you have not shown yourself to others?" asked Torrens.

"Because they were not wrecked as you were," she responded. And that made sense to him, as much sense as sitting there speaking with a woman dead three years.

During Torrens' enforced time on Sable, Amelia showed herself to him again, but only when he visited the hut. She did not know the name of the thief, only that he had come across her body on the beach and helped bury her.

"After he helped bury me, he came back for the ring."

* * *

When he returned to Halifax, Torrens searched for the sealers Ziba Hunt and Coleman Crowell but could not trace them.

Then, many months later, he heard that a sealer living in Salmon River had talked of a ring. Could it be one of the two men? He doubted it, but as he had no other lead, he pursued it, going to present-day Yarmouth.

Torrens arrived in Yarmouth only to learn that though he had found the home of the sealer Crowell, the man was gone, signed on as crew for a fishing schooner off the Grand Banks. Undeterred, Torrens rented a room at the man's home, hoping to either find the ring or be able to trace it. Every morning he would set out to fish the Salmon River, and in the evening he would sit by the fire with Coleman's family. It wasn't until the third day that he made a point of showing them his signet ring.

The mother and daughters each had a turn wearing it, for by then they were quite comfortable with this man staying in their house. They marvelled at the design, and he remarked ever so quietly that he had never seen a ring quite so delicate. One of the daughters disputed that.

"My father brought home a ring once that was ever so fine," she said. Her mother shushed her, but the girl went on, pleased that she obviously had Torrens' full attention. "He got it off a lady that drowned," she finished, flush with excitement.

Her mother cut in. "Don't be foolish," she said. "You know that he traded for it."

"May I see it?" asked Torrens, his calm voice belying his excitement.

"No," said the mother. "He has it with him."

The daughter shook her head. "Oh no, Ma," she said. "He told me he was taking it to Halifax to be sold. He thinks it will fetch a fine price."

Torrens could barely manage to spend another night there, so keen was he to head to Halifax. In the morning he gathered his things and bid them farewell. It would take him a week to return, and he feared the ring would be sold before he could claim it. On the seventh day, he rode along Barrington Street inquiring as to which jeweller would be most likely to have a fine piece for a gift. Having been given a name, he arrived just before closing.

"I am looking for a gift," he said, "a rather fine piece for my wife."

The jeweller showed him two beautiful pieces, a pearl necklace and a gold bangle. But they were not what Torrens sought. "It is to be a special gift," he said. "I have been away a long time and would like something unique."

The jeweller presented a fine filigree necklace. "No," said Torrens. "Do you have perhaps a ring? Something delicate and very feminine. It could have a precious stone but that is not necessary."

"Ah," replied the jeweller, "I think I may have just what you seek. A very unusual piece. Brought in last year by a fisherman from Salmon River who had been left the ring in a will. He would not part with it, but his child is ill."

The jeweller opened a drawer under the display case

and took from it a ring, its fine work a delicate lace of entwined gold. Torrens realized it was the ring described by Mrs. Copeland.

"It is perfect," he said. "How much will you charge me for it?"

"My client would need 5 guineas," he was told. "For his daughter, you know. He would never sell it otherwise."

"I will give you 20 shillings," replied Torrens. This was a far cry from the 5 guineas, or 105 shillings, requested. "If the fisherman disagrees with my offer, he can bring me the finger from which he cut the ring. Then I will pay him in full." With that, Torrens handed the astonished jeweller his card so that the sealer would know where to find him.

Torrens took the ring to the officers' mess and showed it to friends of the Copelands. They confirmed that it was indeed Amelia's.

Now he did not know what to do. Should he take the ring to Sable Island and trust that the lady still haunted the shack? Or should he send it to England in the hope that returning it to her relatives there would be the better choice? It was now the summer of 1804. He would not likely be on Sable again before two years hence, and he did not trust leaving the task to any other. If he sent it to England on the next ship, Amelia's parents would certainly receive it by the anniversary of the wrecking of the *Frances*. Perhaps that would bring peace to the lady.

Torrens sent the ring in the care of a fellow officer and thought little more of it.

But Amelia Copeland did not rest as he had hoped. She continued to frequent the hut until it blew down one year in a winter storm. Denied shelter, she was left to wander the beach, appearing on occasion to the men of the Sable Island Lifesaving Establishment as they patrolled the beaches in search of shipwrecks. She always approached them with her left hand held out, the fourth finger crudely butchered. She never spoke, but it was said that the smell of evergreen lingered long after she had passed, though none grows on the island. Sometimes, a mistletoe berry remained behind on the sand — all that was left of her treasured Christmas kissing bough.

* * *

* While the Copelands' story, including all dialogue, is a re-creation, I have remained as true as possible to the known facts of the sinking of the Frances. *The Copelands did exist, as did all the people who appear in the story. Since my sources identified only Dr. Andrew Copeland by first name, I have ascribed fictitious names to his wife and children in order to better tell their story. The ghost of Mrs. Copeland was last seen in 1947 by a member of the Sable Island Lifesaving Establishment.*

The Kissing Bough

Select Bibliography

Anderson, Dr. William James. *The Life of Field Marshall H. R. H. Edward, Duke of Kent.* Ottawa and Toronto: Hunter, Rose and Co., 1870.

Armstrong, Bruce. *Sable Island: Nova Scotia's Mysterious Island of Sand.* Toronto: Doubleday Canada, 1981.

Butler, Darrel. "A Study of the Evolution of Christmas Traditions in Southern New Brunswick 1780–1885." Working paper, Kings Landing Historical Settlement, n.d.

Campbell, Lyall. *Sable Island Shipwrecks: Disaster and Survival at the North Atlantic Graveyard.* Halifax: Nimbus Publishing, 1994.

Gillen, Mollie. *The Prince and His Lady.* Toronto: Griffin House, 1970.

Herman, Arthur. *To Rule the Waves: How the British Navy Shaped the Modern World.* New York: HarperCollins Publishers, 2004.

Raddall, Thomas H. *Halifax: Warden of the North.* Toronto: McClelland and Stewart Ltd., 1971.

"Royal Gazette." *Halifax Gazette,* June 3, 1800.

Acknowledgments

I would like to thank Wayne H. Moug, Military Curator Parks Canada, Halifax; A. J. B. (John) Johnston, Historian Parks Canada, Halifax; and William Naftel, author, Halifax — three very special people who were unendingly patient in answering questions. Darrel Butler, Curator at Kings Landing Settlement, New Brunswick, helped with the details of Christmas traditions in Atlantic Canada.

Chapter 3

A Spirit of Christmas Past

by Andrew Hind and Maria da Silva

Amanda Martin* had never really considered the line in the Christmas song "It's the Most Wonderful Time of the Year" that refers fondly to scary ghost stories as a cherished holiday tradition. She'd always thought of spirits and spectres as a Halloween convention. What did they have to do with Christmas? Little did she know that in Victorian times — the era recreated at Georgina Village Museum in Sutton, Ontario — it wasn't truly Christmas until a ghost story had been told in the warm glow of a crackling fire. But after one fateful evening, she would never again listen to that song without being reminded of her own haunting Christmas experience.

It was a cold yet pleasant night in December, and with

the feeling of Christmas in their souls, Amanda and her friend Richard Reed decided to visit the Georgina Museum for its annual Old Fashioned Christmas Festival. They wanted to see what Christmas in pioneer times would have been like.

It was their first time at the museum, and they were swept up in the magic of the event. There were no fancy Christmas lights, just the simple glow of candles burning; no fancy decorations, only the ones that had been lovingly made by someone's gentle hands. With the snow lightly falling, the evening had a serene, peaceful feeling to it.

To Amanda and Richard, it felt like they were back in time. Each of the museum's 14 carefully restored buildings was decorated to reflect a 19th-century Christmas. The two friends enjoyed hot apple cider and cookies in a shadowy, lamp-lit log cabin, watched the blacksmith work his trade in his smithy, warmed themselves by the potbelly stove in the Sutton West Train Station, and shopped for presents at the Vanderburgh General Store. Each building was more enchanting than the last. As they wandered around, the tune of Victorian carols filtered out of the one-room schoolhouse, drifting lazily upon the crisp air.

Amanda especially loved seeing young and old alike enjoy the evening, as families left the hustle and bustle of modern life to experience a quieter, purer moment. Back then, it wasn't about the presents. It was about families being together and giving thanks for what they had — being a family was *everything*. The evening reminded her of what Christmas was all about. It couldn't have been more nostalgic.

Finally, the young friends decided to visit the majestic Noble House. Once inside, they could feel that there was something special about this home. They couldn't help but linger in the warm confines of the house, formerly the residence of a prosperous physician, and the most refined building in the village. The place gave the impression that at one time it was host to grand parties. The enchanting sounds of a harpsichord and windpipe added a tranquil tone, and the laughter of visitors gathered around the musicians could be heard all through the house. In that building, more so than any other in the museum, Amanda felt as if she had truly stepped back in time and been issued a personal invitation to a private Christmas party.

Sneaking away from the crowd, the eager friends decided to try a little exploring on their own. Ignoring her better judgment and an uneasy feeling that suddenly consumed her, Amanda quietly ventured to the staircase to make her way to the second floor. At the bottom of the stairs, fright took hold of her, but not enough to convince her to stay behind. She followed as Richard climbed the stairs.

When they reached the landing, Amanda drew back in surprise and her heart skipped a beat. Standing before them in the gloom was a woman dressed in a white Victorian wedding gown. A ghost? A costumed staff member? As soon as her pulse slowed and she came to her senses, Amanda realized it was neither, just a mannequin dressed in 19th-century attire. She and Richard exchanged sheepish grins. After taking a moment to compose themselves, they decided to continue.

At this point, however, Amanda began to feel that their presence was not welcome and that perhaps they should not proceed farther. It was as if they were intruding on someone's privacy. Hugging herself tightly, Amanda shivered in the cold air. Just as she was about to turn to leave, both friends heard a door creaking somewhere in the dark recesses of the second floor. When Richard and Amanda looked at each other, they could see the fright in each other's eyes. Their imaginations began to run wild, creating all sorts of fantastic origins for the strange noise.

But then curiosity took hold. They wanted to see where the sound had come from, and what had made it. Tentatively, they walked down the hallway, looking in disbelief. Not a single room had a door. What had made the noise? Amanda and Richard were *sure* they'd heard a door creaking on its hinges.

At that instant, a strong feeling came over Amanda, more urgent than before, telling her to leave. However, Amanda also felt drawn to the house, as if there was something familiar about it. So she ignored her foreboding feeling and walked to a room that must have been the master bedroom at one time. It was a large chamber, though much of it was consumed by darkness, its details barely discernible.

Amanda almost jumped out of her skin as she saw what looked like a shadow float past the window. The pale look on Richard's face told her he had seen it as well. But it was impossible for there to have been a shadow on the window. They were the only two people upstairs and it was too high up for it to be someone on the outside walking around.

Again, even stronger, Amanda experienced the sense they should leave, a sense she was finding increasingly difficult to ignore. And on the heels of that came an overwhelming feeling of sadness. The emotion wasn't her own, but Amanda was sensitive and had occasionally sensed the presence of people long passed. Although she sometimes couldn't understand the feelings that came over her, she always opened herself up to them, believing there was something the ghost wanted to share. Over time, Amanda would usually unravel the message. That night, she felt she was mourning the loss of loved ones and knew she was tapping into the emotions of some lost soul trapped within this home.

Turning to Richard to tell him it was definitely time to make an exit, Amanda suddenly saw a woman sitting at the foot of the draped bed. She hadn't been there when the friends had entered. Amanda couldn't believe her eyes — the woman seemed to materialize out of the gloom. Amanda's breath felt unfamiliar and heavy in her chest. The woman was a ghost, and clearly one from many, many years ago. She seemed sad and unthreatening, and Amanda couldn't help but notice that she wore a macabre black mourning dress. She wondered who the ghost was, who she was grieving, and why she was in this house. But Amanda also knew that this ghost wasn't about to share these secrets with the living.

Realizing it was time to leave, Amanda took Richard by the arm to grant the spirit her privacy. Quietly and quickly, they snuck back downstairs. On their way down, Amanda shared her vision with Richard in a voice that was as thin as the watery moonlight. Richard was a little shaken, unnerved by the fact that he had been in the presence of a spirit yet had been completely unaware of it.

Once outside and enveloped by falling snow, Amanda and Richard stood and stared at the house in amazement. They had so many questions, but one thing the two knew for certain was that they had intruded on someone's private moment.

The Christmas season progressed, yet amid all the merriment, Amanda's mind kept returning to the Noble House and its spirit. Her ghostly encounter left her sleepless. She couldn't close her eyes without seeing the woman's sad face and mournful eyes. The closer they got to Christmas, the more Amanda began to understand the sorrow that consumed the ghostly woman. She began to wonder if perhaps the sad spirit had actually wanted someone to know the pain and sorrow she was feeling that night. Could it have been the spirit of someone who had lived, loved, and lost within that historic home? Did she lose her loved one around the Christmas holidays, and was she hoping to connect with him once more?

Amanda and Richard knew they'd find no rest — and somehow suspected the spirit wouldn't either — until they uncovered the story behind this haunting. So Richard researched the history of the Noble House, going back to the beginning, to the man for whom the home was named, the esteemed Doctor Charles Thompson Noble. He shared his research with Amanda.

Charles Thompson Noble was born in 1831 on a farm in Markham Township to parents who had emigrated to Canada from the United States some years earlier. He had a privileged childhood relative to that of other youngsters in 19th-century Ontario, received a fine education, and graduated from King's College at the University of Toronto.

For a few years after graduation, Charles gained valuable practical experience as an understudy to his father, also a physician. By 1856, he deemed himself ready to strike out on his own, and headed north for Sutton, in Georgina Township.

When he arrived, Sutton was but a small village. It "wasn't a very large place," Charles would later remember. "The whole town consisted of three hotels, a general store, a few houses and had a population of 180 person." It was a growing community, however, and one with potential. More importantly, Sutton was a community in need of a doctor.

This void meant that Charles was extremely well received when he arrived in town. So much so, in fact, that the community's founding family, the Bouchiers, let the young, single physician use one of their homes as a residence and medical practice. Later, Charles purchased this home, which today bears his family name.

After several years of tirelessly tending his patients, Charles had earned an enviable reputation that made him attractive to men of means attempting to find suitable suitors for their young daughters. He came to the attention of William Johnson, one of the founders of nearby Pefferlaw and a wealthy miller, merchant, and farmer. Johnson was eager to marry his daughter, Margaret Lee, to an upstanding young gentleman, and in the young physician he found a perfect match.

As it turned out, Charles was instantly struck by the beauty and charm of 23-year-old Margaret Lee Johnson and began courting her enthusiastically. Soon, she too fell in love, and the young couple was wed. They settled into married life easily. Charles adored his wife, and Margaret Lee proved utterly devoted to her husband and the family they created. Their first child, Annie Lee, was born on September 26, 1864. Three years later, on September 7, 1867, Charles Jr. was born.

By 1871, Charles seemingly had it all. His family life was contented, his medical practice was flourishing, the community had voted him onto the town council, and he had grown quite wealthy. On top of it all, in late 1872, Margaret learned she was pregnant again. Both she and Charles were ecstatic at the news, and as her figure began to change, their joy became unbridled. Charles couldn't wait to see the smile on Margaret's face when she held their child for the first time; he had seen that magical moment twice before, and both times he had thought he had looked upon the face of an angel.

But when the baby came in April 1873, there were complications. The child, a girl, was healthy, but Margaret began to slip away despite Charles's best efforts. Frantic to save her, he used all of his considerable knowledge and skill. It wasn't enough, though. Margaret Lee, the love of Dr. Charles Noble's life, died on April 10. To honour his beloved wife, the grieving husband named the new baby Margaret. Some say he lavished extra attention on her as a result.

Eventually, the widower remarried, finding a measure of happiness with his second wife, but he never forgot his first love. Their three children kept her close at heart as well, and it was a rare day that went by without at least a passing thought to their departed mother. Margaret Lee Noble's absence was most profoundly felt at Christmastime, however, when families would cross all distances to be together once more. It was at that time, a holiday heavily weighted with nostalgia, when Charles longed most for his lost love.

As Richard's words echoed in Amanda's head, the pieces fell into place, and as they did, her heart began to ache with compassion. It was as if she was feeling the ghost's pain and heartache again. Thoughts began to race through her mind, but they weren't her own. The thought of having it all one moment and then losing it forever the next loomed large, and Amanda instinctively knew that's exactly what happened to the spirit she encountered, a spirit whose name she now knew: Margaret Noble.

Then it came to Amanda. She and Richard were assuming that the apparition she had seen was a woman mourning the loss of loved ones who had perished, but in fact she was grieving her own passing. The loss she felt was that of not being able to share any more memorable moments with her family. The sounds of children giggling, the festive tunes floating up the stairs from the parlour below, and the holiday spirit that seemed to float upon the winter breeze — the very things Amanda and Richard found so magical about that evening at the museum — were torture to this lost soul.

Amanda didn't know why the ghost chose her to share her feelings. Maybe she had been waiting for a sensitive person with an open heart. But Amanda was glad it was her and hoped that having someone who could truly feel her pain could allow Margaret to move forward to the Other Side.

Prior to that visit to Georgina Village Museum, Amanda always thought that ghosts and Christmas didn't mix. After that evening, however, she understood. It will never truly be Christmas until the tree has been trimmed, the turkey has been stuffed, stockings have been hung by the chimney with care, and a ghost story has been told by the fireside.

* * *

A Spirit of Christmas Past

* Amanda Martin and Richard Reed are not the real names of the actual people.

Bibliography

Report prepared for Georgina Heritage by Su Murdoch Historical Consulting, Barrie, Ontario, 2000.

Chapter 4
Adam Brown's Christmas Miracle

by Andrew Hind

Adam Brown had to admit that things looked pretty bad. The weather was foul, as foul as he had seen in his 30 years upon Georgian Bay. Ice clung in sheaths from the lighthouse he tended, angry waters crashed against the sides of the tiny island, and dark grey clouds hung low and ominous in the sky.

It was Christmas Eve 1903. He was alone in the lighthouse, three weeks after he was due to be taken off the godforsaken rock. But the prospect of spending the holiday season alone was not what was weighing most heavily on his mind. Instead, Adam was more concerned with remaining alive. Would he live to see the new year, or would he be one more victim claimed by Georgian Bay?

Adam looked out at the water and contemplated its cruel fury. Hidden from view just below the azure waters was a sinister danger that had claimed dozens of lives over the years. Granite shelves, rocks, and shoals lurked beneath the waves, an ever-present danger that was at odds with the region's beautiful scenery. The skeletons of numerous vessels, such as the *Jane McLeod,* the *Midland,* and the *Seattle,* littered the lake bed.

Guiding vessels through this maze of rock was a string of lighthouses occupying isolated islands. Theirs was a thankless but necessary task. Without these lighthouses and their indomitable keepers, the roll call of ships and crews sent to a watery grave would be too lengthy to recount.

Probably the most forlorn of these beacons of hope was that at Red Rock Island, 10 kilometres north of Parry Sound. Since its founding in the 1850s, Parry Sound has been the area's largest and most important port. Tens of millions of board feet of logs and cut lumber passed through it on a yearly basis, feeding the insatiable appetite of ever-growing cities along the American east coast and midwest.

After several schooners sank nearby at terrible cost in men and material, it became apparent that vessels entering Parry Sound desperately needed navigational assistance. The need was so critical, in fact, that generally tight-fisted sawmill owners contributed half the cost to the first lighthouse, built in 1870.

This first lighthouse was wiped away by one of the fierce

winter storms that often plague Lake Huron. A second light-house was erected on tiny Red Rock Island, but it too suffered at the hands of Mother Nature and had to be replaced within a few short decades. However, this was the lighthouse that Adam found himself in that fateful Christmas Eve.

Exposed to the full force of the elements, the lighthouse was constantly battered by wind and waves. In wintertime, the entire structure was shrouded in a coating of ice as the lake crashed against the rocks and threw frozen spray into the air like an angry geyser. A person would be hard pressed to find a more claustrophobic, desolate location than the Red Rock lighthouse.

Tending such a location takes a special breed of man. He must be dedicated, willing to withstand the endless months of monotony, and able to endure the rigours that come with existing in this harsh environment. Lighthouse keepers are a hardy breed, and Adam Brown was the hardiest of the lot. He was a legend in Parry Sound.

Originally a fisherman operating from the nearby Mink Islands, Adam was a veteran mariner, well acquainted with the tempers of Lake Huron and hardened to her oft-times harsh climate. With the demise of the local fishing industry in the late 1890s, he took up the job as lightkeeper at Red Rock, existing alone on the Rock from the time the spring break-up of the ice signalled the start of the navigation sea-son until late November, when winter once again closed the lake to shipping.

Adam Brown's Christmas Miracle

The first five years had been relatively uneventful. In 1903, that changed suddenly and dramatically. Even as Adam stood at the window on Christmas Eve and contemplated his future with the storm raging outside, the year had already proven memorable.

Winter's full wrath had come early that year. In fact, by the end of October, several weeks earlier than was the norm, Lake Huron had been closed to most sane traffic. Only the largest and sturdiest vessels, commanded by the most experienced or foolhardy skippers, ventured out upon the swells after the calendar turned to November.

On November 10, the steamer *Seattle* found herself out upon the lake. Her fires were blazing red-hot as the captain sought to coax every last ounce of speed from her engine. Behind him, ominous black clouds roiled low in the sky. A storm was bearing down on Georgian Bay, and, in the captain's experienced eyes, it was going to be a vicious one. He silently prayed to see the reassuring glow of the Red Rock lighthouse on the horizon, for then the safety of Parry Sound Harbour would be near at hand.

It was not to be, however. The gale overtook the struggling 48-metre steamer on the morning of November 11, while she was still about 60 kilometres north of Parry Sound, and when it struck with its full fury, the *Seattle* immediately found herself overwhelmed. With her holds full of lumber, she was sluggish at the rudder and rode low in the water. Waves crashed over her deck, threatening to sweep the crew overboard. Pumps struggled to keep pace with the water pouring into her hull from atop deck.

Then, to the crew's horror, the *Seattle*'s engines suddenly failed. Now they and the steamer were at the storm's mercy. Wind and waves crashed against the ship, driving her inexorably toward the jagged Mink Islands. With a deafening crack of splintering timbers, she was run up against a shoal just offshore of Green Island.

The steamer was grounded with such force that seams immediately began to open in her wooden hull. Water poured in unhindered. For a time the overworked pumps managed to keep up, but the churning waters constantly ground the ship against the rocks, tearing the hull to shreds. Soon, water was pouring into the hull faster than it could be pumped out. The *Seattle* was doomed. The seasoned crew, trying to hide their mounting fear, watched helplessly as water rushed into the holds.

Thankfully, the storm abated enough for the crew to launch lifeboats and reach the relative safety of Green Island. There, from the shore, they watched as the *Seattle* slipped beneath the waves to her watery grave.

But they were not out of danger yet. Green Island is isolated, uninhabited, and desolate. With little in the way of shelter and no food or water, the captain and his 10 crew members knew their survival depended upon someone willing to brave Georgian Bay's storm-tossed waters and dangerous shoals. It was a dreadful task, one requiring a stout heart and a wealth of experience.

As time passed and no rescue vessel appeared on the horizon, the stranded men began to despair for their survival. All were soon convinced that Green Island would become their collective tomb. None, however, had counted on the heroism of Adam Brown.

Despite the harsh weather, Adam, upon spotting the stranded crew, took to his little skiff in a daring attempt to rescue them. The fierce wind and enormous waves conspired against him, tossing the would-be saviour and his boat about with abandon. Adam braced himself and pulled on the oars with all his strength, ploughing relentlessly through the roiling surf. Several times the boat was driven ashore on a rocky island, and over the groan of the wind, Adam was sure he heard a horrible tearing sound of the hull ripping open.

Incredibly, both the boat and its builder survived the ordeal, arriving battered but unbroken at Green Island to rescue all 11 members of the *Seattle* crew and return them safely to the mainland. Thanks to Adam, these sodden men lived to bask in the warmth of family Yuletide festivities just over a month later.

But after the rescue, Adam found himself in a situation as desperate as the one the *Seattle*'s crew had faced just a few weeks earlier. Indeed, even more perilous.

Adam was to have left the lighthouse for winter quarters in late November. But the ship that was supposed to pick him up hadn't arrived on its scheduled date. Nor did it arrive the next day, nor the day after. The weather was too foul to risk an entire crew to rescue one man. Days turned into weeks, and still Adam remained a prisoner on Red Rock.

Come Christmas Eve, Adam no longer held out any hope of rescue. The ship that was to have picked him up was almost a month overdue, and he doubted one would come now that the lake was a daily maelstrom. No, he thought, I have to get myself off this rock, and I have to do it now.

A frown stretched across Adam's weathered and creased face. It was hardly a suitable day to be out on Lake Huron. The waters were not yet solidly iced over, but the angry whitecaps bore chunks of ice that had broken off from the ice forming along the shore. The lighthouse reached up toward a dark, foreboding sky, and the air was crisp and biting, cold even for December. Nevertheless, with food, fuel, and hope all but extinguished, Adam realized that he didn't have the luxury of awaiting ideal conditions. If he was going to attempt a break for shore, he'd have to do so now, while he still had his strength and endurance.

By this time the lighthouse was sheathed in ice, looking more like a frozen stalagmite than a navigational aid. Adam had to chop his rowboat free from its encasing, expending valuable energy in the process. It was a small victory when at last the boat was released, but when Adam leaned over the railing to lower the boat, his heart sunk. The ice that covered Red Rock had formed into razor-sharp ridges and jagged spear points that were sure to rip the bottom out of the boat as Adam dragged it toward the open water.

Wiping the sweat from his brow, Adam retreated inside the lighthouse to formulate a plan. He had been in tight spots during his fishing days, so he wasn't overly concerned yet. Besides, to panic would be to cloud his mind and senses when he needed them sharper than ever. Adam scurried down to his workshop and quickly inventoried his tools and equipment. With a trained carpenter's eye, he decided he had the time and equipment to fashion a jury-rigged derrick that would allow the boat to be safely carried over the ice.

He worked feverishly, realizing that with each passing hour, he was one step closer to death. Finally, after a few hours the ad hoc derrick was complete and ready to be put to the test. To Adam's relief, it worked perfectly, and in short order the rowboat was bobbing in Georgian Bay's cold waters. Hopes buoyed, the stranded lighthouse keeper climbed aboard the tiny craft and set his eyes upon the shore 10 kilometres away.

I can do this, he assured himself. After all, I know the lake and her moods like no other. She's a cruel mistress, but I've tamed her many times in the past and I can do so again.

Adam shoved off from the lighthouse that had been his prison for the past three weeks and began to row toward the distant mainland. Adrenaline pumped through his veins for the first half hour, helping him cut through the white-capped waves that threw the rowboat around as if it were nothing more than flotsam. As time passed, the short-lived rush of energy drained away, and exertion began to take its toll.

His arms and back ached from the repetitive strain. Healthy and in good weather, the hardened seaman would have found the distance to be covered a simple jaunt, but in his weakened state and in atrocious weather, it seemed epic. Water sprayed over the bow, freezing within the boat and upon the form hunched at the oars. Wind and waves worked against him, and the biting cold pierced through his layers of clothing to sap his energy.

Crunch. The rowboat suddenly ran up against something solid. Adam spun on his seat and saw, to his dismay, an ice field that stretched as far as his eyes could see. If it had been a solid ice shelf, he wouldn't have been concerned. He could simply have climbed out and walked. But this was an entirely different matter — an endless expanse of free-floating drift ice that rose and fell with the waves. Occasionally the floes would come together with an unnerving crushing sound, but in general they were separated by several metres of threatening water.

For hours Adam probed along the edge of the drift ice, looking for a place his boat could pass through. Finally, he decided that his search was futile. There was no way through, and to tempt fate by trying to force a passage could end in disaster. His boat could become lodged between sheets of ice or, worse, be overturned or crushed into splinters as the sheets drove into one another.

Adam had no choice but to get out and walk across the ice, jumping from one floe to another.

Lord, give me the strength to see this through, Adam silently prayed. Without divine intervention, he was no longer confident he'd live through this ordeal.

Gathering up his courage, Adam stepped out onto the ice. Behind him, he dragged the rowboat. It would have been easy to leave the boat behind, but it would also have been shortsighted. After all, he might need it to cross a stretch of water, or to shelter him for the night. Besides, it was government property and therefore it was his sworn duty to bring it in.

Putting one numb foot after another, Adam began to trek across the ice floes. His pace was slowed by the weight of the boat but, worse, he was often forced to backtrack when he came across a stretch of water between floes that was too wide to leap across. When no other floe presented itself, he had to wait until the tide brought them closer together.

Leaping from one ice floe to another was terrifying. A misstep could result in his being plunged into bone-chillingly cold waters in which survival would be measured in a matter of minutes. Even if he could somehow pull himself from the watery grasp, he would certainly perish from hypothermia shortly thereafter. Adam knew well the dangers and was cautious. Nevertheless, he was aware that much of his fate was out of his control. An ice floe might be unstable and shift under his weight, tossing him into the water. Or the ice might be thin, unable to bear him. Waves could cause the ice to suddenly rip apart. His strength might fail at any time.

After an hour or so, Adam was relieved to find himself standing upon a solid sheet of ice that stretched all the way to the rocky shore ahead. He had travelled three kilometres, and another seven separated him from salvation.

By the time the sun was high upon the horizon in the early afternoon, the weather had begun to change for the worse. The sky turned steely and the temperature dropped rapidly. A frigid wind whipped up the waters behind Adam in an icy froth and swept in ominous, heavy clouds. Soon, snowflakes began to fall.

Turning up the ice-crusted collar of his frayed coat, Adam bent into the wind, driving himself into the gathering storm. With each excruciating step, he began to believe more and more that he should have waited at the lighthouse for the tender to arrive, or for a better day to make his bid for escape. Doubt began to seep in, diluting his faith.

Still he pressed on, struggling against the storm and his own fatigue. His hands and feet were now completely frozen and nearly lifeless, and his face was left raw and stinging by the bitter gusts of wind.

What bothered Adam the most, though, what truly frightened him, was that his 41-year-old body was giving out. Subsisting on a single biscuit a day for two weeks had rendered him a shadow of the robust man he had been.

He realized now, too late, that he was far weaker from the reduced rations than he initially thought and was in fact in no condition to undertake such an arduous voyage. It was nothing short of a miracle that he had made it even this far, but his body could take him no farther.

I'm going to die out here, he finally admitted to himself. I'm going to die out here on the very lake upon which I've spent my whole life. And on Christmas Day, no less.

Overwhelmed by the realization, Adam felt what little strength he had suddenly drain away, as if someone had sucked it out with a bilge pump. Exhaustion washed over him, an exhaustion so complete he was powerless to resist. He wanted to sleep so badly, even though he knew to do so would be fatal, but after a brief inner struggle, Adam lay down on the ice.

Just a few moments of rest, that's all I need, the light-keeper convinced himself. In truth, his thoughts were becoming cloudy, blurred, as cold and fatigue ate away at his consciousness.

Adam was nodding off to sleep when suddenly he was jolted awake by sounds carrying across the bay. At first he couldn't make them out, but then he came to believe they were voices.

Out here, on Christmas Day? Adam thought. That can't be. No one would be away from their family on Christmas to ice fish. It's just the wind playing tricks on me.

But was it really? Adam couldn't be sure whether he was

in a delusional state and imagining the voices, or whether they were real. If there were people out on the bay, he might yet be rescued.

I'm not ready to die. I have to believe, Adam said to himself.

In desperation, and mustering up all the feeble strength he had, Adam put two fingers in his mouth and blasted three sharp, shrill whistles. Perhaps the sound would carry far enough that someone would hear it.

A kilometre away, on a desolate, windswept island, three ice fishermen huddled in a drafty shanty, seeking the warmth of a potbelly stove. By chance, one of the men happened to duck outside to draw some water from the lake and heard what sounded like faint whistles playing upon the wind — three distinct blasts, the maritime signal for danger. The fisherman raced to the highest rock on the island and scanned the horizon.

There. Out on the ice. He saw what he was sure was a rowboat and, to his horror, what looked like the prone figure of a man stretched out beside it. The fisherman raced back into the cabin and alerted his friends, and together they hurried out onto the ice.

Adam was slowly losing his battle. But then he heard voices again — this time, he was sure of it. He feebly lifted his head to look. There, rapidly approaching, their dark forms starkly outlined against the white background, were three figures.

Adam Brown's Christmas Miracle

Three. Like the magi who were directed to Bethlehem by God in the Nativity stories. Adam smiled feebly at the magical coincidence of it. And like the wise men of legend who brought Jesus gifts of gold, frankincense, and myrrh, these men were giving him a gift as well — the gift of life.

The fishermen did indeed save Adam's life that Christmas Day. Within the hour, he would have succumbed to the cold. Immediately upon seeing the ice-caked figure prone on the ice, the men knew how close to death's door he was. Gingerly lifting Adam from the ice, they carried him back to the cabin as swiftly as they could. There he was wrapped in blankets, placed beside the fire, and fed the first real food he'd had in weeks. Then he gave in to the blissful embrace of sleep.

In the cabin's warmth, Adam drifted in and out of his slumber. Whenever he awoke, he heard men talking, and even once, he was sure, he heard carols and hymns being sung in the dim, red glow of the fire. The voices were raspy and coarse, and those speaking the words were wrinkled and weather-worn. His saviours were hardened outdoorsmen. But to Adam, they were beautiful angels.

Bibliography

Butts, Edward. *Guiding Lights, Tragic Shadows: Tales of Great Lakes Lighthouses.* Toronto: Thunder Bay Press, 2005.

Holiday Misadventures

Gutsche, Andrea, Barbara Chisholm, and Russell Floren. *Alone in the Night: Lighthouses of Georgian Bay, Manitoulin Island, and the North Channel.* Toronto: Lynx Images, 2003.

Chapter 5

Aglow with Holiday Fear

by Andrew Hind and Maria da Silva

B eing young and in love, when passion often overtakes rational thought, can sometimes make your mind imagine strange and unexplained things. This might have been the explanation for the horrifying account told by a young couple who only had eyes for each other, if many others had not also reported similar experiences.

One winter evening in 1963, a Newfoundland teenager — a member of the Meade clan from Summerford — decided to take his girlfriend on a quiet drive through the countryside. It was to be a night like so many others they'd shared together.

Except this was Candlemas Day, an ancient holy day

commemorating the date that the infant Jesus was brought to the temple. According to Jewish law, this had to be 40 days after his birth — February 2. So impressed with the Christ Child was Simeon that he declared the infant "a light to lighten the gentiles, and so light is the theme of the day." It was a Candlemas light that would make this a night like no other the two young lovers had shared.

The evening began normally enough. The young man often drove to the nearby hamlet of Pike's Arm to the home of his girlfriend's family, the Burts. This night, as usual, he eagerly piled into his car and headed north.

Despite the dangers of a snow-covered road, he found it hard to keep his mind on the road ahead. Instead, his thoughts were filled with visions of his girlfriend, her scent, her touch. He couldn't think about anything else other than the time they would share together, and the drive passed quickly. Before he knew it, he was pulling up in front of her house.

His sweetheart was just as eager. Each moment of waiting was torture as her stomach did nervous flips and her heart raced with excitement. She already had her coat and boots on, so by the time the familiar old car pulled in front of her house, she was racing from the front door. The car had barely stopped before the girl was in beside her beau.

Greetings were exchanged and then they were off. Neither of them spoke during the drive; they didn't need to. Instead, the boy gently reached for his beloved's hand and the warmth of it trailed up to her heart. It was as if the two of them knew what each other was thinking. The love in their eyes said everything, telling each other that the night would be memorable as always.

They drove to their usual spot, a little-used road skirting the nearby bog, and parked the car on the shoulder. As it always was, the road was deserted. There was not another vehicle to be seen and not a home for kilometres, just as the sweethearts had hoped. They quickly became lost in each other's arms, and time seemed to stand still.

He was the first to notice it, a bright light rising from the bog and floating slowly toward the car. Realizing that her boyfriend had become distracted, the young woman turned to see what had captured his attention. Then she, too, saw the mysterious light.

At first, they thought they were imagining things, that their eyes were playing tricks on them. But the light was definitely moving. Coming closer. Growing larger. It was blinding. The closer the light came, the more frightened the couple became. Their eyes strained to penetrate the glare and see what exactly it was that was approaching them, but to no avail.

Now the light was directly in front of the car, shining through the windshield. The couple shrunk away from its intensity as dread built inside them. What *was* it?

Something about the light reminded them of a lantern being held aloft, bobbing in the darkness as its wielder groped through the darkness. Thinking that there might be someone in trouble and in need of assistance, the young man cast aside his fears and decided to confront the person.

The girl didn't want him to leave her side. She was terrified that something might happen to him and that she'd be left alone. She pleaded for him to stay in the car, but he was determined and pulled away from her clutching arms. Giving her a reassuring smile, he climbed out of the car.

Tentatively, the young man walked around front to stand before the light. "Do you need help?" he asked with more confidence than he felt. Something felt wrong, unnatural. "Are you hurt or lost?" His stomach formed a cold knot beneath his ribs.

There was no response — not a sound. Instead, the light flew directly toward the boy, causing him to duck quickly out of the way. The brilliant orb sailed past him to the rear of the car, hovering there silently. Rather than go around the vehicle, it seemed to have gone right *through* it. Then, as quickly as it had appeared, the light simply vanished before his eyes, as if swallowed up by the night.

There was not a soul in sight. Once again, the teenagers found themselves alone on the deserted road.

Terror jolted through the young man's body. Nothing of this world could have floated through a car and simply disappeared. His heart racing with fear, he ran back into the car, bewilderment etched on his face. Frantically, he locked all the doors to ensure they were safe from whatever it was out in the still of the night. He froze, and tried to stifle the sound of his own ragged breath so his girlfriend wouldn't be more alarmed than she already was. But he was stunned by what he had experienced. His mind simply couldn't comprehend what had occurred.

The two young lovers looked at each other in shock. The fact that the light was gone didn't make them feel any better, nor could it slow their racing pulses. What if it returned?

It was time for them to leave.

Speeding back to the girl's house, they couldn't wait to share their experience with her parents. But would anyone believe them?

As they told their story, swearing that every word of it was the gospel truth, they were relieved to hear that they were not the only ones to encounter the strange light. In fact, many others had in the past — sightings of the eerie glowing orb had become something of a Christmas tradition in the region, appearing especially frequently on or near Candlemas Day.

* * *

Although Candlemas Day marks the final day of the sacred Yuletide season, it isn't only a day of religious observance. Traditionally, it was also one of joyous festivities, with singing, dancing, drinking, and an expansive meal. As soon as this final party of the holiday season had drawn to a close, all decorations and ornaments were taken down and Christmas greenery burnt.

By the 19th century, Candlemas Day had largely become obsolete around the world — rarely noted, let alone celebrated. In Newfoundland, however, Candlemas Day has always been considered the last hurrah of the Christmas season and is usually accompanied by a big celebration.

The girl's father told them the tragic tale of one such late 19th-century celebration, when a man died and the legend of the Candlemas light was born.

The story goes like this.

While the locals of the hamlet of Cobb's Arm were enjoying themselves in the warmth of their community lodge, the weather turned fierce. It wasn't a concern at first because the party would last well into the night. Perhaps the storm would blow over by then, they thought.

But it didn't. In fact, it got worse. As the party wound down during the wee hours of the morning, many revellers decided not to risk the storm. Instead, they would huddle together in the lodge and wait out the blizzard.

There was, however, one man who would not wait. One can only imagine why this man would risk his life to venture out on such a foul night. Perhaps he was thinking only of his wife and children, fighting to keep warm in their tiny cabin, without their husband and father. Whatever his reason, the front door creaked open as he prepared to leave. The blizzard was so bad that it howled like a banshee, drowning out the shouts of the people urging him not to go. However, his mind was obviously set, so he probably wouldn't have heeded their warnings even if he had heard them. It took a brave man — or a foolish one — to venture into a raging blizzard on a night as dark as pitch.

Within seconds, the lodge disappeared from his sight, swallowed by a shroud of white. The man attempted to make his way home, but the snow came down so thickly that it was impossible to see anything in front of him. All landmarks disappeared. The world simply did not exist beyond the feeble glow of the lantern he held before him. He had no means of navigating, no way of determining which direction to walk.

The man attempted to quicken his pace just to try to keep warm. But he couldn't have travelled very far before starting to feel the cold wind cut through his clothes like the sharp lashes of a whip on his trembling body. Desperately, he continued his journey, but with numbness setting in on his feet and hands, he began to fear for his survival.

Finally, his strength started to fail. Knowing now that he wouldn't reach his destination, he found it difficult to find the will to continue his forlorn journey. If only he hadn't been so stubborn and had listened to the others. If only he had remained in the warmth of the lodge. Now, every agonizing inch he moved forward only made him realize he would never see the ones he loved again.

Just as his hope was giving out, so, too, was his lantern. Though it was only the tiniest of flickering lights, inadequate in the face of such dense, driving snow, the lantern's glow was the only companion he had that night. When the flame began to die, his hopes were extinguished with it. The man knew he couldn't go any farther and dropped to the snow.

Though all the energy was drained from his body, he could still feel the icy cold take hold of his near-lifeless body. Relief from the suffering came only when his eyes finally froze shut and he breathed his last frosty breath.

Morning came and all the revellers filed out of the lodge. But the merriment of the night before was soon drowned out by the sobs of a despondent woman. Her husband — the man who had left the party — had not made his way home. Word spread and concern mounted. The community came together to form a search party, hoping that he might have taken shelter in someone's home, barn, or woodshed.

After hours of searching, they finally discovered his frozen body in the depths of a nearby bog. He was contorted by the icy grasp of death, the moment of his passing captured in his rigid features. The searchers' hearts sank as they saw that his arm remained outstretched, the lantern still held aloft in clenched, white fingers. Did he hope, in his last desperate minutes, that someone might see the meagre glow of the dying flame and come to his rescue? Was he still hoping that somehow it would guide him home?

If one believes numerous eyewitnesses over the century and a half since this man's death, the answer is a resounding yes. Since that tragic night, many people besides the two young lovers have seen a ghostly light floating over the bog, wandering aimlessly over the barren landscape. Most believe the light is that lost soul still searching for his way home. Appropriately enough, it is most often seen on or near the anniversary of his death — February 2.

The sudden crackling of the fire brought the young lovers out of their thrall. Neither had realized that the girl's father had finished his story and was now sitting back in his chair, silent and thoughtful. As fear clutched their hearts like icy talons, the teenagers gripped each other's hands. For them, rather than simply signifying the end of another Christmas season, February 2 would always be associated with terror.

* * *

While the Candlemas light signified only terror for that young couple, other people like to think of the light as a beacon of hope. One such story happened around the 1940s.

With a frightful blizzard rolling in, a young widow living near Cobb's Arm became a frenzy of activity. Shutters were closed and latched, the fire was stoked, livestock secured in the barn. She knew she needed to do the many things that her husband had once looked after.

She was only recently widowed, the love of her life having been presumed lost at sea during the war. Now she was solely responsible for herself and her children, and it was a heavy burden. She came to depend more and more on her eldest son, a boy of about 10. The woman knew that she expected a lot from someone as young as he was, but she wasn't able to care for her three younger children without his help.

So it was that when the mother realized that firewood needed to be stocked up to keep the home warm during the cold evening ahead, she didn't hesitate to ask her eldest to see to it.

Knowing well his responsibilities as the new man of the house, the boy did what he could to help his harried mother. He felt his father's absence as much as any of the children, but found strength in his new role. He had to grow up quickly.

So on this day, with the wind blowing wild outside, he opened the door to make his way to the woodshed like he'd done many times before. Even though he was young, he knew that the storm would blow through the cabin as if it were made of paper, so it was important to keep the fire well fed and the home warm until the blizzard died down. That would take a lot of wood, so he'd have to make several trips.

With each trip, the storm grew more fierce, the snow more blinding.

It was a few minutes after he had disappeared through the door on what he promised would be his last trek to the woodshed that his mother began to have a sick feeling in her stomach. Her son should have returned, and the storm outside seemed to growl with increased anger with every passing minute. When she threw open the door to call for him, she discovered that the snow had picked up so much that the woodshed, which was only a stone's throw from the house, was no longer visible.

Regretting having let her son go out in the blizzard, the woman grabbed her wrap and whistled for their dog, a shaggy mutt that was the family's true friend in times of danger. She hoped that if she, too, got lost, the dog would guide her safely back home to her other sleeping children. Fearing the worst, she stepped out into the cold of the night and went in search of her wayward son.

Maybe he was huddled up in the woodshed, waiting until there was a break in the storm and the house was visible once more before attempting to return. But when she reached the shed, she found it empty. Her thoughts turned for the worst, imagining the boy wandering alone in the blizzard, scared and crying for his mother, slowly succumbing to the cold. She couldn't bear to lose another loved one.

The woman summoned all her courage to continue the search for her child, ignoring the cold she felt biting through her body. She was a mother on a mission. But as the snow fell more thickly, she began to despair that she would ever find him. Hope receded quickly.

Then, all of a sudden, out of the dark, a blinding light appeared from the direction of the nearby bog. It looked as big as a full winter moon, and it seemed to float slowly through the night. A surge of warmth spread through her body. Thinking it was her son's lantern, she raced toward the light. Her dog, usually so fearless in the face of any danger, seemed restless and began whining. He dragged on the leash, only reluctantly following his master toward the glowing orb.

Desperate to reach her child, the woman carried on. All of a sudden, the orb came to a stop, allowing her to catch up to it. Her heart sank when she realized the light did not come from her son's lantern. Instead, she saw in the pale glow an old man standing before her. She stepped closer, and as she did, fear took hold. The frightened woman looked to her dog for protection, but it was as if he had been frozen to the spot.

Drawing closer to the mysterious person, she noticed his deathly white complexion and hollow eyes, and almost fainted with fright. When he began to reach for her with frozen fingers, she clenched her eyes shut, hoping that it was all a hallucination from the cold. A few moments later, her eyes opened to reveal the image slowly fading. When the spectral figure had disappeared, it took the mysterious glow with it.

All her emotions caught up with her as she looked in disbelief at the spot where the spirit had stood. Tears filled her eyes when she saw her son huddled against a tree, right where the spectral man had stood mere moments before, his lantern long since extinguished. Rushing to her son's side, she took him into the comfort of her loving arms. The woman knew she would never have found him if she hadn't followed that mysterious bright light.

All over the world, Christmas is the season of light, a

symbol of Jesus as the light of the world and of the hope He represents. Is the ghostly Candlemas light of Newfoundland another expression of this age-old symbol — or is it a lost soul doomed to forever spend the holiday season alone?

Bibliography

Jarvis, Dale. *Haunted Shores: True Ghost Stories of Newfoundland and Labrador.* St. John's, Newfoundland: Flanker Press, 2004.

Chapter 6
Christmas in Captivity

by Andrew Hind

t was Christmas Eve 1837, but there were other things on Captain William Johnson's mind than holiday cheer.

He stood by the window of his study, watching as a frigid north wind swept in ominous, low clouds off the lake. Icy snowflakes began to fall, and soon Oldcastle, his magnificent manor home in Upper Canada, was enveloped in a shroud of white. In William's native Scotland, Christmas Eve was known as Oidhche Choinnle, or Candle Night, and as was customary on that holy evening, William sparked a match to light the candelabra resting upon the window sill. He was loath to do it, however, and did so only because to do otherwise would be to alarm his young ones. Surely they'd question why Papa hadn't lit the candles that would guide the wise men on their way to visit Baby Jesus. William was apprehensive, however, worried that the lights would guide the way of men with far less holy intentions.

Even here, far away from the provincial capital of York (Toronto), news had spread about the rebellion and the clashes that had settled the matter. The army of reform-minded peasants, seeking only to force an equitable division of power among all classes, had been crushed mercilessly. William felt a tinge of regret. He was strongly opposed to violent revolution and had spent his entire naval career opposing one. But it was no secret that he sympathized with the plight of those who sought change in Upper Canada's governance. Too much power and wealth rested in the hands of too few privileged individuals.

William knew it was these sympathetic views that might now get him in trouble. At church earlier in the day, he had heard whispered talk about the vigilante bands scouring the countryside in search of rebels in flight and those suspected of aiding and abetting the uprising. Anyone who had ever voiced any support for the Reform movement was now cast in doubt. William worried that he might be next on the apprehension list.

His musings were shattered as the door to the study burst open. A young girl with dark hair, a beautiful smile, and wide, black eyes came running toward him.

"Papa! Papa! Dinner's ready. It's time to eat!"

William knelt and the little girl ran happily into her father's arms. His worries shunted aside, William returned the youngster's hug, kissing the girl. He combed a stray hair away from her angelic face.

"I'll be right along," he said as he gently guided his beloved youngest daughter to the door. A painful lump formed in his throat. A myriad of emotions squeezed his heart as he watched her go — pride, love ... and fear that this might be the last Christmas he would spend with her.

Composing himself, William followed his daughter into the expansive dining room, a chamber decorated with the finest furnishings available in colonial Canada. Taking his seat at the head of the table, he looked upon his family with pride. His wife, Roxanna, was beautiful and refined, the envy of many a man in these frontier parts. Together they had seven children, ranging from 13-year-old William Jr. to little Janet, just 3 years old. He beamed widely as the children took their chairs, fidgeting anxiously for the time when they might dive into the feast before them.

Christmas had been widely banned in Scotland centuries before, but in some households — the Johnsons' included — the traditions were carefully handed down through the generations. For William, it was a time to appreciate all he had built for himself in Georgina Township, along the shores of Ontario's Lake Simcoe. He had wealth, he had status, he had a fine home and thriving businesses, and most importantly, he had a large and healthy family.

Christmas in Captivity

Every Christmas, the Johnson family sat around the ornate dinner table and enjoyed a feast like no other. William would stand at the head of the table and make a stirring and heartfelt speech, his oratory skills honed by years of inspiring men upon the eve of battle. After the old salt had at last taken his seat, the family would dig in.

The table would be topped with the most tempting sights and the air filled with mouth-watering aromas. There were golden pies, shortbreads, fruitcakes, marvelously tasty black buns and sweetly aromatic athol brose, a whisky-flavoured oatmeal concoction. Perhaps the most anticipated treat was a boiled pudding called clootie dumpling, in which one would find good luck tokens secreted by Roxanna during preparation.

This year, William performed his annual rite by saying a few words about privilege, loyalty, family, and faith. However, with the uncertainty of the rebellion casting a dark pall over the holiday, the words more than ever came straight from the heart. He then led his brood in bowing their heads in prayer, thanking the good Lord for all their blessings.

"Amen," he concluded, giving his children the nod that told them the feast could begin.

No sooner had grace been said than the doors burst inward. Wisps of snow coiled into the manor, followed by more than a dozen armed men — pro-British vigilantes — wielding pistols, muskets, and axes.

The intruders barrelled into the dining room. Cutlery

clattered onto china plates as the startled children recoiled in fright and Janet began to cry. Roxanna let out a sharp cry as pistols were waved in her husband's face, then she recovered and moved to comfort her children.

In spite of all the chaos around him, William remained calm. He had faced shot and sword in numerous battles during his youth, and now his combat instincts came flooding back. Like all great military leaders, he had always been able to make calculated decisions in the midst of confusion and violence. On previous occasions, this ability had helped secure victory, but today it would save his family.

A stocky fellow with an air of authority strode forward and eyed William belligerently. "You are wanted on suspicion of treason to the Crown," he announced smugly. "You will come peaceably, lest your children witness your death."

Though William remained outwardly calm, his heart and mind began to race. He briefly considered wiping that smug look off the fellow's face with a swipe of his fist. He also eyed the sabre mounted on the wall, mentally calculating whether he could reach it before lead poured into his body.

But saner thoughts prevailed. His main objective in life was to protect his family — he would die for them. If he refused to go peaceably, if he put up a struggle, his wife and children might be hurt. Neither did he want them scarred by the sight of their husband and father being killed before their eyes. He had seen enough death in his military career to know that one never truly gets over the experience. It wasn't something he wanted them to have to struggle with.

No, William thought, this is a battle I cannot hope to win. It is better to capitulate than sacrifice oneself in a forlorn cause.

Calmly, he pushed his chair back and stood. He nodded to his family, ordered the children to be strong, told Roxanna he loved her, for perhaps the final time, and then offered himself over to the vigilantes. Taking no notice of the sanctity of the holiday or the crying children, the cold-hearted posse dragged him from his home.

Christmas dinner went cold. No one had any appetite. All of the season's gaiety had vanished with William.

* * *

As the darkness of his cell enveloped him and the hours of the night ticked slowly by, William not only pondered the uncertainty of his immediate future but also reflected on his life, career, and the events that led up to his current travails.

William Johnson was born at Chirnside, Scotland, on September 19, 1784. He was the product of a wealthy family with a long history of military service, most especially in the Royal Navy. He entered adulthood at a turbulent time in European history, an era that saw the continent wracked by the French Revolution and the Napoleonic Wars.

During many of these dark years, it seemed nothing

stood between Britain and defeat save the Royal Navy and its dauntless officers. Among the thousands of sailors serving aboard His Majesty's vessels and safeguarding the nation was William Johnson.

William had entered the navy in 1801 at the age of 17, serving as a midshipman in the English Channel and then the West Indies, where he was involved in the capture of French island possessions. On many occasions, Midshipman Johnson took sabre in hand as a member of the landing parties. Later, he served with distinction in European waters, earning praise for his leadership, bravery, and seamanship.

Despite his years of notable service, in 1813, William, by then a lieutenant, was put on half pay and retired from active service. The war was nearly won, there was no longer a threat from the French navy, and Britain began to downsize her forces accordingly. A career military man, William found himself out of sorts. Forced to find a new path in life, he decided to take advantage of the government's offer of free land in Upper Canada for newly retired officers.

He set sail for "the colonies" in 1819, but the adventure hardly began auspiciously. The voyage across the Atlantic, which typically took six weeks, was plagued by terrible storms and instead lasted three agonizing months. After landing in Montreal, William had to walk all the way to York and then to Georgina, an exhausting trip that took almost six months.

William set to work establishing a homestead on his 1000-acre land grant, building a simple log cabin and clearing land for crops. Shortly after, he dammed a nearby river and built a sawmill along its banks. Unfortunately, a severe storm led to flooding that swept all his hard work away. Undeterred, William rebuilt the mill. In time, he added a flour mill and woollen mill to his holdings.

Despite being a wealthy and refined man, William Johnson didn't seem to fit in well with the other aristocratic, well-to-do landholders that dominated Georgina Township's social order. In fact, he was very nearly ostracized by them. For one, he was Scottish instead of English. More importantly, he took the extremely unpopular stance of supporting his friend and fellow Scotsman William Lyon Mackenzie in his movement to reform the corrupt government of Upper Canada.

By 1837, Mackenzie began to despair over the lack of progress, so he and his followers prepared for the time when force might be required to make their point heard. By year's end, the situation was worse. The pent-up fury erupted into rebellion in early December, when a ragtag army of poorly armed farmers and craftsmen marched on the capital along Yonge Street.

News of the uprising sent the province into a panicked frenzy. Citizens armed themselves to defend their homes and the honour of the Crown. Vigilante bands of pro-British citizens began springing up to arrest suspected rebel sympathizers. People began to suspect their neighbours of treacherous activities. It didn't matter if one took up arms or not; anyone voicing displeasure with the government or support for the Reformers was automatically under suspicion.

Lack of popular support was the uprising's downfall. There were too few rebels, and they were too poorly equipped. The fighting ended quickly with Mackenzie's defeat at Montgomery's Tavern on December 7. The rounding up of suspected insurgents, however, continued for weeks.

It was in this environment of suspicion and hysteria that Captain William Johnson found himself abducted. His only crime had been to express some sympathy over the years for the cause of the Reformers.

* * *

William was tied uncomfortably to a chair. His arms, bound tightly behind him, were dead asleep. His back ached, his legs were cramped. But the discomfort he felt inside was far greater than what he felt outside. He didn't know what his fate would be, whether his wife would soon be widowed and their children left fatherless. He didn't know whether his name would soon be soiled by false charges, leaving his family ostracized in their adopted homeland. Perhaps worse, he didn't even know what had befallen them after he had been escorted from his home. Had they been tormented or abused? How were they holding up? The unknown tortured his mind.

The old mariner felt his bowels tighten. He felt more

like a hunting trophy than an officer in Her Majesty's Royal Navy, and it angered him. Like all prisoners of war, William felt his dignity threatened. He could survive interrogation or even physical abuse. But without pride, he would have nothing, even if set free. Rank and medals were the outward recognition of courage and honour, but these qualities could be compromised by captivity.

William had only his faith to combat these uncertainties. He was sure that God wouldn't abandon him on the day of his own son's birth. Surely the Holy Spirit would be at his side on this holiest of days.

Several hours later, an interrogator entered the room. His legs still bound, William started to rise. The captor pulled a gun and aimed it at him. He pointed for William to stay. Still, the bound officer struggled to stand. William was a navy officer, a proud man with decades of service. He humbled himself before no man, save a superior officer or the queen, and his captor was neither. As he struggled to get his feet under him, he continued to stare into his captor's eyes. He noted the man's bravado waver just a bit.

Before William could get all the way up, he was thrust back down. Still, he sat with his shoulders squared and his chin raised. His pride was intact and would remain so despite the imprisonment and the questioning.

For two days William was grilled. Did he render aid, material or otherwise, to Mackenzie's cause? William did not hide his affection for his fellow Scotsman but staunchly maintained his loyalty to the Crown. Did he not in that past speak words supportive of the Reformer movement? Did he know where Mackenzie had hidden himself? Where was he during the skirmish at Montgomery's Tavern?

The interrogation came in barrages, often with the same questions, only worded differently each time. Were they trying to catch him in a lie? Wear him down? Or did they simply not like the answers they were given? Probably a combination of all three, William surmised.

Despite lack of sleep and food, which ate away at his mental facilities, and the exhausting routine of questioning, William refused to break. Every time he found his will sapping, he thought of his family. He shored up his flagging strength with fond memories from Christmases past, holding on to these precious images as one would a life belt in storm-tossed seas.

On December 27, after two days of incarceration and questioning, William was led from his holding cell and released. The inquisitors had either tired of their game or become convinced of their prisoner's innocence. In either event, William was free to return to his family.

He could hardly contain his joy as he emerged into the daylight. Despite the bitter cold and falling snow, a distinct warmth washed over him. He marvelled at the familiar feeling welling within him. It was the same giddy excitement he felt on Christmas as a young boy so many years ago. For the first time in countless years, he was reminded of what it was like to experience the magic of the Yuletide season through the eyes and spirit of a child.

With youthful energy, William raced for home. When he saw Oldcastle, the knot that had formed in his stomach during his imprisonment vanished, allowing him to breathe easy for the first time in days. He noticed the candles burning in the windows. Like beacons, guiding me home, he reflected. William suddenly felt an affinity for the magi who were guided to the bedside of the Baby Jesus more than 1800 years before. A revelation swept over him. This feeling of divine joy, of the sanctity of family and loved ones, is what Christmas is all about. It was a humbling experience.

The door opened and out piled his wife and children. William saw fear and fatigue in Roxanna's eyes, and the tears that she had stoically fended off for two days suddenly overwhelmed her. William scooped her into his arms, hugging her. The sob that racked his chest and the warm tears that dampened his cheeks surprised him. Some old warhorse I am, he thought.

He then knelt and tugged his children into a tight circle. He felt as much as heard the deep sigh that shuddered through every one of them. He echoed their sense of relief.

A family reunited. It was undoubtedly the finest Christmas present any of the Johnsons ever received. They had missed spending Christmas Day together, but realized that the old cliché was right after all: it's not the day that counts, what's important is being together.

With his family all around him, and tiny Janet cradled in his arms, William felt the tears flow down his beaming face. He finally understood the true magic of the season — and it was a blessing.

Bibliography

Frim, Monica. *Secrets of the Lakes: Stories from the History of Lake Simcoe and Lake Couchiching.* Toronto: Lynx Images, 2002.

Thompson, Ruth. *Pefferlaw: The Johnston Family and Friends.* N.p.: Self-published, n.d.

Chapter 7
The Christmas Eve Cathedral Killing
by Rich Mole

A merry Christmas, indeed, Victoria City Police constable Bill Irvine likely grumbled as he pulled on his pyjama pants. Of all the nights! On this wet and rainy Christmas Eve 1890, he should be at home, or his parents' home, a friend's home — *anybody's* home. Instead, he was turning down the cover of his cot in this Spartan little room in the police barracks. While other off-duty officers had been making the rounds of saloons and hotels, Irvine had been making his own rounds — of the city's jail cells. That was a sobering duty any night, but especially so on this festive night. Well, duty calls, Irvine reminded himself. No candlelit Christmas tree in the corner for Constable Irvine. No happy squeals of excited children.

The thumping on the other side of his door interrupted Irvine's thoughts.

"Come in," the policeman called out.

The door opened, and a wet, shivering man strode a few paces into the room, stopping halfway between bed and door.

"I came to give myself up," the clearly inebriated stranger announced. Irvine's brow creased in confusion. What was the man babbling about?

"I'm the man who shot the man tonight," the stranger continued evenly.

Oh, Lordy, another Christmas Eve reveller, Irvine sighed to himself. Earlier, the downtown streets had been full of them, tooting their little horns and ringing their little bells. But the man's speech wasn't so slurred that Irvine had mistaken the visitor's words: *shot* the man?

Irvine pulled on his boots, took the visitor by the arm, told him he was arresting him, and, still clad in his pyjamas, walked him to a nearby cell. It was turning out to be a strange Christmas. Just how strange, Constable Irvine could not have imagined.

Home for the Holidays

A few days before, David Findlay Fee had packed his suitcases for the short voyage from East Wellington down to Victoria. The general store he managed was in capable hands. In any case, the store would be closed Thursday and

Friday — Christmas Day and Boxing Day. After one busy day on Saturday, it would be closed again for the Sabbath. The employees could muddle through until his return.

Managing the store for the past year had been a good experience, a chance for Dave to prove himself, but, oh, how he missed the city, his friends, and all those good times. In East Wellington, a coastal coal village near Nanaimo, life — if you could call it that — was a far cry from the bright lights of Victoria, where Dave had grown up. If he timed it just right, there would be precious little opportunity for his parents to hand him an apron and push him behind the counter of the family's busy corner store. That would be just fine. This was his holiday!

Dave would drop his bags at his family's home, hug and kiss his parents, say hello to his brother, and be off to find his firefighter friends around the main fire house. He missed those Tiger Engine volunteer practices almost as much as he missed the camaraderie of his fellow red-shirts. He might even run into the affable chief, Tom Deasy. Dave would share a few pints with the gang he'd known since the days with the Young Men's Institute and play a little billiards with some of his Knights of Pythias brothers. They would be anxious to bring him, their former chancellor, up-to-date. A party, a concert, dancing with the ladies, who knew what else?

Oh, yes, and come Christmas Eve, Midnight Mass. Of course, this time, it actually might take place inside the new St. Andrew's Cathedral. It had been 10 weeks since he had attended the Catholic cathedral's cornerstone laying. A resplendent occasion it was, too. The man in charge of decorations, Fire Chief Deasy, had seen to that. The cathedral should be just about finished now, Dave figured.

Plans for the cathedral had been delayed over and over again. When last in Victoria, Dave had heard that a shortage of workers had forced organizers to advertise for labourers from Seattle and San Francisco, for heaven's sake. Fenians, too, it was rumoured. *There* was trouble! Those rabble-rousing Irishmen seemed hellbent on spreading their hatred of the English to their new homelands, instead of leaving it behind on the old sod, where it belonged. They were a blight on the rest of Victoria's Irish community. But banish those thoughts, Dave chided himself — this is Christmas!

A New Job in a New City
About two months before Dave set off, a recent arrival from the United States, armed with a letter of introduction from a stonemason in Seattle, stood quietly before St. Andrew's stone contractor, John Harbottle. The contractor didn't know how long he could use another man on his crew. After all this time, the building would finally be finished. However, extra hands would hurry the work along. He took Larry on.

At first, Larry was happy enough. He had found a new job in a new city. He had also found a place to live close by — the Dominion Hotel — where he shook hands with two other hotel residents and cathedral construction site workers, Edward Bermudiz and labourer John Crawford.

Soon, Larry was reunited with a Seattle friend, Joseph Silk. Like Larry, Joe was working on the cathedral, but he lived in a small cottage right across the street from the construction site. A month after he had arrived, Larry had had enough of the hotel and was rooming with Joe. Yet, in spite of a new job and new-found friends, he chafed with a deep-seated discontent.

In preparation for the cathedral cornerstone laying, someone had strung up a little flag on a construction derrick. A beautiful flag it was, the Stars and Stripes really, but bordered in lovely green and overlaid with a beautiful little harp, revered symbols of Irish patriots. What better place for it, Larry had thought, than the town's new Catholic cathedral? Soon, all kinds of decorative flags would be flying near the cornerstone.

Then someone — that uppity fire chief, Tom Deasy, someone claimed — came huffing along in his long, white rubber raincoat and ordered the flag down. And him an Irishman, yet! Of course, Deasy didn't do the dirty deed himself. He got a Frenchman to haul it down.

Larry rescued the flag from the pile of bricks where it had been tossed. Soon, people saw him strutting about with the flag over his shoulder. Before long, it was up again — and then torn down once again. Larry was incensed enough that he told Joe he would talk to the bishop about the incident.

One night not long after the cornerstone flag incident, after a few drinks at the Dominion Hotel, Larry stood morosely at the bar and began to replay the episode.

"Three cheers for the American flag!" he shouted, lifting his half-empty glass.

Across the room near the fireplace sat John Crawford. To the half-drunk Crawford, Larry's slurred shout was more of a challenge than a toast.

"Three cheers for the British flag!" John shouted back across the crowded room. Within minutes, the exchange became heated, but, as usual, both men ended up shaking hands and sharing drinks together at the bar.

Then, just a few days before Christmas, the construction all but complete, Larry was laid off. The despondent worker was told to see Aeneas McDonald, the foreman of the carpenters. Aeneas was also responsible for hiring watchmen. Edward Bermudiz had given Larry a hair-raising account of a recent after-dark incident. Both Edward and Aeneas had heard noises from inside the church, whooping and hollering and what sounded like construction barrels being tossed about.

"Someone wants to do some mischief," Edward told the foreman. He grabbed a lantern and walked around to a side entrance to investigate. Just as he was about to enter — where had McDonald got to? — he spied some shadowy figures in the half-light.

Edward decided to take no chances. He threw the lantern at the nearest one, connecting solidly. The intruders ran from the scene. Later, Edward was shocked to discover that the man he had hit was Aeneas McDonald himself! The boys were still laughing about that one. It was Edward's first and last night as watchman.

Was McDonald up to his old tricks? Larry wondered. Edward and others had told him about the foreman's peculiar habit of playing after-hours pranks on his watchmen, scaring the living souls out of them with phony intrusions. Was this the kind of work he really wanted? Was McDonald a man he wanted to work for? The answer was obviously no, but Larry had little choice.

On Wednesday afternoon, December 24, Larry talked to Aeneas about a night watchman's position. Aeneas told Larry he could start that night. Lovely, Larry must have thought, now I'm to work Christmas Eve.

"D'ya have your gun?" Aeneas sneered as he turned away. "Bound to be ghosts around, y'know …"

"I haven't got a gun myself," Larry admitted loudly as his new boss wandered off. "But I know where I can get one." Aeneas seemed not to hear.

Armed and Dangerous

Edward Wrigglesworth was tending bar in his father's saloon early that Christmas Eve when Larry Whelan sauntered in and asked Wrigglesworth for the loan of his double-barrelled shotgun and a few cartridges. Wrigglesworth was a little puzzled by the request, but Larry was a familiar face and, as there were no cartridges for the weapon, the request seemed harmless enough. Larry appreciated the gesture, and so bought himself a drink.

When Edward Bermudiz opened his hotel room door and saw Larry standing there with a shotgun under his arm, he simply smiled. Here was one night watchman who wasn't going to be cowed by pranksters. Larry had come to borrow Edward's umbrella. The request certainly made sense. It had been raining off and on all day, and he knew it was going to be a long, wet night for Larry.

The umbrella wasn't going to be enough to ward off the chill on this damp Christmas Eve, so Larry decided to fortify himself with a drink or two downstairs. A few minutes later, he stood admiring the weapon he had propped against the bar. He picked it up. How did the American rifle drill go? He hoisted the gun vertically against his chest and, to the amusement of those in the room, began to mimic the rifle-drill movements. John Crawford, who was among the crowd watching the performance, walked over. Perhaps Larry would like to see some *real* rifle drill — British rifle drill. Larry smiled good-naturedly and handed him the gun. John stomped and strutted up and down, hefting the shotgun this way and that. This was thirsty work and so the Dominion Hotel's "parade square soldiers" decided to have themselves another round.

John had spotted the rags squeezed into the end of the

gun muzzles and knew they were there to keep the rain out. Breaking open the gun, he also noted with some curiosity that both chambers were empty.

"What's the gun for anyway?" he asked.

Larry told him it was for his protection on his first night as watchman at the new cathedral. He motioned upstairs and reminded John of Edward's embarrassing run-in with Aeneas McDonald and his pranksters.

"If he comes around playing tricks on me," Larry announced, "I'll give him a charge of shot."

As John watched Larry weave his way out into the stormy night a few minutes later, John turned to a couple of acquaintances.

"The gun's not loaded." He grinned conspiratorially. "Let's go 'round and see him."

To the others — warm and dry and content to stay that way — the invitation was less than appealing.

"C'mon! We'll have some fun with him!" John urged. There were no takers, so when John Crawford left the Dominion, he walked out on his own.

Joe Silk was sitting quietly enjoying his pipe when Larry stumbled into the cottage. Joe's eyes widened when he caught sight of the gun.

"Where's that cartridge bag of yours?" Larry asked.

Joe gestured over his shoulder. "It's hanging on the wall, but they're all empty I guess."

Within seconds, Larry was pawing through the cloth

bag with a drawstring. He turned to Joe. "There's something in this one," he said, holding up a cartridge.

Joe shrugged. "Then it's a blank. I gave all the loaded ones away."

Larry held up another.

"They're both blanks; they'll never hurt anybody," Joe insisted, puffing away on his pipe.

A few minutes later, Larry had left the cottage to stand his watch around the cathedral. Soon after that, Joe decided he needed some tobacco for his pipe, turned down the lamps, and left the cottage.

With a new pouch of tobacco inside his pocket, Joe was walking swiftly through the drizzle — wanting more than anything to be snug and warm by the stove — when he heard laughter and noticed some men standing on the sidewalk up ahead. He realized, even in the half-light, that one of them was Larry. How many other men would be carrying a shotgun on a city street near midnight on Christmas Eve?

Walking up, Joe then recognized John Crawford. John was capering about like a schoolboy, chuckling under his breath, acting the fool, as usual. Larry was standing stock still, glaring at him, his shotgun in the crook of his arm. The sound of an organ floated across the street from the temporary cathedral, where the faithful had begun to gather for Christmas Mass.

"I'm goin' in there," John teased, jerking his head in the direction of the darkened cathedral.

Joe was becoming uneasy. Larry was tipsy enough to do something foolish. And what if one of those "blanks" in the gun turned out to be a live cartridge? Better safe than sorry. Joe yanked the pipe from his mouth. "Don't go in!" he yelled at John. "The gun is loaded!"

John glanced at Joe. "It's not loaded," he cackled. "I was looking at it …" Joe's silence cut his laugh short and he turned to grim-faced Larry, who was now pointing the gun straight at him. John stepped toward Larry. "Larry, let me see."

John wrapped his hand around the barrels and pulled on the gun. Larry jerked the gun back. Stepping closer, John moved his hand swiftly up the barrels, searching for the release. In an instant, the barrels swung down. John's heart began to hammer as he stared at the brass ends of two shotgun shells snugged into the barrels.

"Take them out!" he grunted and reached up to remove the shells. Larry pulled the gun back and snapped it closed. He stood expressionless for a moment, gun held tightly to his chest, and, without a word, turned and walked toward the cathedral.

"You'd better take those cartridges out of the gun, Larry, and go home!" Joe called after him. "Let the church take care of itself. I wouldn't stay out tonight for five dollars!"

John pointed a finger at Joe. "You'd better try and get that gun." He turned in the direction of the cathedral and swallowed hard. "Larry's pretty drunk." Joe blinked in silence, watching John's breathless nervousness, marvelling how that taunting idiot of a few moments ago had disappeared. "He ... he might fall down," John stammered. "That gun could go off and he might shoot himself or ..." He turned again to Joe, "... or somebody else."

Joe's uneasiness grew. And if the shells in that double-barrelled shotgun *weren't* blanks? If something should happen, he would never forgive himself. Joe could see that John was pretty nervous. That was good. The more frightened he became, the easier it would be to convince him to simply leave. His continued presence might provoke Larry into doing something rash. Perhaps, Joe thought, he could hurry John along.

"Oh, by God, yes!" Joe cried, making John even jumpier. "If anyone comes around here and raises a row, Larry *will* shoot him. If he don't shoot, well ..." He stared hard at John. "Well, God damn me!"

Joe then assured John that he would go inside the building after Larry. That seemed to do the trick.

Satisfied that he had fobbed off the job of controlling Larry, John walked rapidly away toward his hotel. But Joe had no intention of going anywhere near his drunken friend. When John was out of sight, he simply headed for the warmth of his nearby cottage.

At about the same time, Dave Fee and his buddy Frank Partridge were stumbling out of the temporary cathedral. Having enjoyed a grand night at the masquerade party at the Philharmonic Hall, they had left the fun, briefly, to put in an appearance at Midnight Mass. The sudden appearance of two young party goers in frivolous costumes — long, white coats trimmed in gaudy, red braid — was enough to provoke some quick, disapproving glances in the cathedral. The newcomers endured the unspoken criticism for two or three minutes, then Frank nudged his friend and the two slipped outside again.

Joking and jostling each other, the Christmas revellers stumbled arm in arm down to the corner, Dave's little golden trumpet bouncing at the end of the chain around his neck. They turned in the direction of the Philharmonic Hall, anxious to rejoin the others in their final merrymaking. Suddenly, a dark forbidding figure holding an umbrella and what looked like a walking stick of some sort loomed in front of them.

"I challenge you!" a voice boomed out in the rain.

Dave looked up. "What's that?" he asked. Then the figure thrust the walking stick up and pointed it at Dave.

At the blast that followed, Dave clutched hard at Frank's arm and collapsed on the sidewalk, pulling his pal down with him. Rain streaming in his eyes, Frank tried to make out exactly what had happened to his friend.

"Dave? Dave?"

There was a large hole in the front of Dave's costume, and blood was quickly darkening its shiny white fabric. When Frank looked up, the shadowy figure was gone, and an umbrella lay on the sidewalk.

Joe was sitting near his stove a few minutes later when a dripping, dishevelled Larry Whelan walked in and stood before him, gun in hand.

"I'm afraid I've hurt someone," Larry said calmly. Joe watched him walk to the corner, lean the shotgun against the wall, and turn to face him. "I had to do it to save myself."

Hurt, Larry had said. In Joe's mind, the more accurate word was *shot*. What he had feared had actually happened. Joe told Larry that the best thing he could do was go to the police station and give himself up.

"All right, put on your hat and come down with me," Larry said.

A few minutes later, as they plodded along to the jail, Larry had second thoughts. Perhaps he was being hasty. He needed advice, he told Joe. Kindly John Harbottle would know what he should do, he thought.

The two men eventually located the cathedral contractor at the Monarch Saloon, enjoying some Christmas Eve cheer. When he heard the story, Harbottle was incredulous. Larry, clearly drunk, didn't even know if he had actually hurt anyone or not. Telling the two to wait for his return at his house, Harbottle hurried off in the direction of the cathedral to verify Joe and Larry's crazy tale.

A few minutes later, an ashen-faced Harbottle was back from the busy crime scene. It was true. Give yourself up, he advised Larry. Larry urged the men to go along with him. Anxious not to be implicated further, Harbottle told him it would be better if he went alone. That suited Joe. Outside Harbottle's door, Joe saw his friend off and hurried home.

When Joe stepped into his little cottage after an absence of less than two hours, he found it full of policemen. The officers had broken in the back door and ransacked the place. They took the evidence they discovered — the shotgun and cartridges — into their custody, along with a loudly protesting Joe Silk.

Murder's Aftermath

On Victoria's gracious Cook Street, not far from the gentle hills of oceanfront Beacon Hill Park, Chief Justice Sir Matthew Baillie Begbie looked out of the back windows of his comfortable home and brooded. Beyond the sheltering veranda and the leafless trees that hugged the spacious house, the broad flat lawns — tennis court lawns — lay soaking and silent. Bereft of nets and summertime guests, the empty green lawns were a mournful sight in the incessant drizzle. There had been no gentle, white snow this Christmas and, since Fee's murder, not much cheer, either. Like this city, nature herself seemed to be in mourning. Ghastly deed, perpetrated outside a house of worship — and such ironic timing! So be it. Brutal murderers had never shown respect for time or place.

The judge hadn't known David Fee or his family, but if the stories in the *Daily Colonist* were any indication, the engaging young man would be missed. Tomorrow's funeral was likely to be a big one. The newspaper on the dining room table also carried the details of the coroner's inquest.

Whatever had possessed the police superintendent? At the inquest, the man blithely suggested that "it was unnecessary to call medical evidence," as he had testified to the cause of death.

The judge had read the passage with disbelief. Happily, the attorney general, Theodore Davie, had stepped in and had the province's most esteemed physician, Dr. John Helmcken, hurry off to undertake a hasty post-mortem, albeit *after* the fact. The judge didn't like that one bit. The inquest should have been over the day it began, but now it was bound to stretch on into next week. Begbie chafed at unwarranted delays. This inquest might very well take as long as the trial itself. And who knew when the trial would begin? There was something else his lordship didn't like.

During the first day of the inquest, the prisoner had decided to act in his own defence, actually cross-examining the men he had caroused with the night of the murder. Unconscionable! What the devil was this fellow Whelan playing at?

Years before, Begbie had seen others in the docket practically convict themselves because they inadvertently destroyed their own case. "Didn't I tell you to keep your mouth shut?" Begbie had thundered from the bench at a "helpful" prisoner who all but admitted he was at the crime scene in question. Let the fate of the accused be determined on the evidence or testimony presented, not out of his own mouth or through his own bumbling attempt at jurisprudence.

However, there might yet be one positive outcome from the prolonged inquest. By the time the trial actually began, perhaps Whelan would have found someone to defend him properly. After all, Victoria wasn't some Cariboo gold-rush camp. The judge wouldn't be holding court on horseback, trying some case of petty larceny. This was a capital case of cold-blooded murder, tried in the Court of Assize in the capital city of British Columbia!

It was to be another two long weeks before the judge found himself presiding over the Lawrence Whelan murder trial. By that time, January 16, 1891, Larry had indeed found counsel. Begbie should have been pleased. However, the first thing Larry's lawyer did was request an adjournment, telling the fuming judge that he needed time to familiarize himself with both his client and the details of the incident. Crown counsel wasn't happy with the delay, either. Under the circumstances, however, there was little else Begbie could do but grant the request. It appeared this trial was going to be a prolonged affair, after all. It would not resume until January 30.

On that day, the outraged and mournful and merely curious jostled one another noisily for courtroom seats. Explaining the cause of death, Dr. Helmcken painstakingly traced the path of internal destruction, past numerous shattered bones and a severed blood vessel to a piece of lead embedded in the victim's shoulder. A parade of other witnesses took the stand: police officers, Edward Bermudiz, Frank Partridge, Fire Chief Tom Deasy, John Crawford, and a decidedly nervous Joseph Silk.

Much was made of the cornerstone flag fiasco. Was this a murder or a political assassination? The evidence to support the assassination theory was flimsy, at best. A man lay dead, but the motive for the killing remained a mystery. Could it be that, in his drunken stupor, Larry simply mistook an innocent man's masquerade party costume for the fire chief's long, white raincoat? Both coats were produced as evidence. Was David Fee simply the wrong man at the wrong place at the wrong time?

When prankster Aeneas McDonald was examined, onlookers understood why Larry Whelan had placed so much importance on being armed that fateful night. Yes, the foreman admitted, he had asked the prisoner if he had a gun. It was a joke, he insisted. If Whelan had actually been carrying a gun, the contractor added hastily, glancing nervously at the judge, of course he would have taken it from him.

"It is barely possible that your asking the prisoner if he had a gun might have produced all the trouble," Begbie shot back before ordering a brief adjournment in the proceedings.

In the courtroom and corridor outside, noisy speculation was rife. On that dark and rainy night, were McDonald's pranks enough to provoke a drunken, frightened man to pull the trigger? many wondered. Others scoffed. There *had* to be more to it. That young, likable Dave Fee should die a victim of nothing more than a twist of bizarre Christmas Eve fate seemed inconceivable.

The debate raged on after the day's testimony was completed. It mattered little to Joseph Silk, who was understandably more concerned for his own well-being than deducing a motive for a crime he most assuredly had nothing to do with.

When Joe took the stand, he immediately had the crowd's attention. He refused to testify until the charge against him — accessory to murder — was dropped. Begbie reminded him that all he had to do was refuse to offer any comment that might intend to incriminate him. At his lawyer's urging, Joe declined the offer. The crowd watched as the debate raged between the defence and prosecution. Finally, the attorney general broke the deadlock.

"Under the facts at present possessed by the Crown," Davie told the judge, "I have no intention of proceeding with the case against Silk. If he gives his evidence freely, he will be allowed to walk out of the court a free man."

This was all Joe needed to hear.

After Joe's lengthy testimony — the shells, the gun, the conversation in front of the cathedral with John Crawford, Larry's confession after the shooting — Begbie announced that he could see nothing that would justify holding Silk, and he was discharged.

"I thank your Lordship." Joe beamed and took a seat

among the spectators to a heartfelt round of noisy foot stomping and applause. That was too much for Begbie.

"Who's keeping order in this courtroom?" he demanded of the nearby police sergeant.

"The sheriff," the sergeant answered.

"Well, Mr. Sheriff," Begbie admonished him, chiefly for the benefit of the crowd, "if you see anyone causing a disturbance in this courtroom it is your duty at once to arrest him and bring him before me." Then he turned his glare to the crowd and proceeded to admonish them as well.

Larry's attorney announced he did not propose to call any witnesses. The law did not allow Larry to give evidence on his own behalf. That was unfortunate. If allowed, the accused might have been able to explain his actions.

The attorney general ridiculed the defence, who had insisted that Larry was "not an assassin, but a dangerous fool." As for the weapon, and the plea that Larry "did not know it was loaded," Davie continued, "the papers were full of this old story day after day."

Justice Denied

After the long and exhaustive summations that afternoon, the jury retired to reach a verdict. Much to Begbie's surprise and displeasure, the 12 men were back inside the courtroom within an hour. "If the shooting was done; with intent to do grievous bodily harm and resulted fatally, would that be murder?" the jury foreman asked.

"Most certainly," Begbie replied.

At 5 p.m., the jury was still out. Here was trouble, Begbie must have thought, as he adjourned the court until 11 that night. Yet, just four hours later, the jury was back in the packed courtroom, with an anxious Larry sitting in the dock, awaiting their decision. Begbie ascended the bench and read that the jury had found that Whelan had shot Fee "with intent to do bodily harm, but without premeditation."

"I cannot accept this verdict!" Begbie announced. "How can it be without premeditation and still be with intent to do bodily harm?" he asked incredulously. "It is not a verdict and I again must ask you to retire."

As he waited anxiously for this particular jury to come to some sort of sensible conclusion, Begbie likely recalled other troublesome jurors. After one incredulous acquittal, the judge had scribbled in his bench book, "The ignorance, prejudice and stupidity of the juryman is the privilege of the prisoner." Good men and true they might be, but jury members had often sorely tried his patience.

Once again, at close to midnight, court was reconvened.

"What say you?" the clerk asked the jury.

"We find the prisoner guilty of murder, but unpremeditated."

"That is no verdict at all," Begbie complained to the foreman. "The killing must have been premeditated to make the crime murder," he explained. Obviously, this particular jury needed even more guidance. "Was he guilty of murder or of manslaughter or are you in favour of acquittal?" the judge told them, quite plainly giving them their options. He consulted his pocket watch. "It is now within five minutes to 12. I will have to either dismiss you before midnight or keep you until Monday."

Leaning this way and that in their seats, the members of the jury whispered tensely among themselves. At two minutes to midnight, the foreman arose once again.

"We find him guilty of manslaughter."

"Are you unanimous in your decision?" the judge asked.

"We are."

Larry Whelan breathed an audible sigh of relief.

On Monday morning, the chief justice opened his bench book, reached for his pen, and began to write the notes he would refer to in court in a few hours. Manslaughter? When the crime was so clearly an act of murder? The jury's verdict amounted to justice denied. The man should be hanged. But if a jury thought otherwise, so be it, Begbie concluded angrily. A magistrate was allowed certain latitude in cases of manslaughter. Begbie was going to exercise that latitude to the very limit.

"As to manslaughter," Begbie explained to the court later that day, "a judge might commit to prison for an hour or a day, or impose penal servitude for life."

In the dock, Larry Whelan held his breath.

Begbie went on to state that Whelan was a "quarrelsome fellow" who was "anxious to have trouble." When the prisoner tried to defend himself, the judge silenced him swiftly. Finally Begbie pronounced, "I am as convinced that you stand there, guilty of willful murder, premeditated all along, as I am of my own existence!"

Begbie had more to say, much more. He made a mockery of the suggestion that Whelan's willing surrender was a sign of his humanity. The judge allowed that Whelan was no better than a cunning, sheep-killing wolf when, chased by dogs, he "fled to the feet of the farmer and implored him to save him."

The judge's voice grew more intense. "If the jury had taken proper care of the lives of their fellow citizens, they would have found a verdict against you." How long, Begbie asked, would the farmer banish the wolf to a zoo — a week or a month — just so he could come back and destroy the flock? "So I must deal with you," Begbie said.

"Never again will you be allowed to call yourself a free man; never again will you be allowed to go on your drunken brawls," the judge's voice rumbled in the hushed courtroom. "Never again will you carry your flag over your shoulder and challenge a fight; never again will you *shoot down* like a dog, an estimable young man, a worthy citizen." He paused and took a breath. "I have not in thirty-two years upon this bench, been called upon to pronounce the sentence which in this case I must. Believing you guilty of willful murder, I will protect you from the dogs. You shall not be torn to pieces by your indignant fellow citizens."

At last Begbie reached his sentence. "You shall go from here to be made miserable, to be a slave for the rest of your life. You are not going to a home, an asylum, a refuge; but to prison, where you shall work without hope of freedom or reward, for all the days of your life. You must live as an example that men cannot carry on their drunken lawlessness with impunity; a man's life shall be protected! The sentence of this court is that you be sent to penal servitude for the rest of your natural life!"

Larry collapsed in the dock, his sobs echoing inside the silent courtroom. Then, as the judge rose to leave the courtroom, uniformed officers lifted Whelan to his feet and led him away.

Scarcely three years after mourners had paid their last respects to David Fee, another large funeral procession wound through the streets of Victoria, as a grateful city laid the esteemed chief justice, Sir Matthew Baillie Begbie, to rest.

Almost exactly 10 years after he had been sentenced to life behind bars, a prisoner was released from the penitentiary in New Westminster. Lawrence Whelan was free to celebrate Christmas 1910 in any way he wished. The wolf was at large again.

The Christmas Eve Cathedral Killing

Bibliography

Adams, John. *Christmas in Old Victoria.* Victoria: Discover the Past, 2003.

Allinson, Sidney. "Murder Outside the Cathedral." *Times Colonist, Islander,* December 18, 2005.

Paterson, T. W. "Fee Felled by Cowardly Act." *Times Colonist, Islander,* December 22, 1991.

Williams, David R. *The Man for a New Country: Sir Matthew Baillie Begbie.* Sidney, BC: Gray's Publishing Ltd., 1977.

Various articles from *Daily Colonist,* December 1890, January and February 1891.

Chapter 8
Merry Murderous Christmas
by Rich Mole

For almost every person living in the Yukon between 1897 and 1899, the gold rush years were the strangest of times. Every Christmas endured during those years was a strange one. For most of the dreamers and schemers who had abandoned homes, families, and jobs during the Klondike gold rush, December 25 was just another date on the calendar. And for most men huddled near the richest creeks on earth, Christmas merely meant a shot of carefully hoarded hootch and another plate of beans shared with grizzled partners in dimly lit one-room cabins.

A game of cards was poor defence against the Yuletide invasion of bittersweet memories of the life and loved ones left behind. Outside, where each day knew no sunlight for weeks on end, a bleary-eyed man might stand silently in ash-smeared snow, marvelling at the bands of red, green, and blue light dancing in the sky above and wistfully remember other Christmases …

Christmastime Travellers
Given the bleak circumstances of the Klondike, it was little wonder that men of means decided to journey "outside" to share the holiday season with family and friends. However, it was no snap decision. The trip meant days of treacherous travel in the dead of winter over hundreds of kilometres of barely broken, snow-covered trail that wound down to the coast across a chain of frozen lakes.

For Fred Clayson, the end of the Yuletide trail was Skagway, Alaska. There, near the muddy streets of the coastal boom town, Fred would walk into the outfitters' warehouse and shake hands with his brother and partner, Will. It had been months since the two men had seen each other. Will was expecting him, and Fred anticipated that a fine old time would be had. They richly deserved it.

Separated by a huge tract of wilderness, each brother had worked hard to make the wholesale business a success. The loaded scow Fred and his employees had navigated down the Yukon River months before had been unloaded on Front Street by eager Dawson City merchants and traders, who would pay almost any price for the valuable merchandise on board. Fred's most important Christmas present to his brother would be the profits made in Dawson.

Yes, the Clayson brothers had a lot to celebrate. Which is why, in a merry mood, Fred had already bought himself a Christmas present. He had managed to purchase one of the newfangled contraptions called a bicycle, a rarity in the Yukon. This was no ordinary bicycle, but a like-new 1897 Columbia model. Nothing but the best, Fred was proud to boast to others who laughed and shook their heads. Determined to go "outside" in style — wherever and whenever the trail allowed — Fred decided he would pedal his way to the coast.

For Lynn Relfe, Skagway was only the halfway point on his journey home. He wouldn't clap eyes on his family until the steamer docked in Tacoma, Washington. But the trip was worth the cost, because Lynn, too, had plenty to celebrate — he was still alive. That sweltering summer of 1899, in the overcrowded town where raw sewage still floated in the alleyway muck and poisoned some of the water, Lynn had twisted and turned in the delirium of typhoid, like dozens of others. He had managed to survive. Others hadn't been so lucky.

Thanks to his lucrative job as cashier and bookkeeper at the New Pavilion, the former bartender could easily afford the trip. The opulent combination of saloon, gambling house, dancehall, and theatre was a magnet for money. Into his pack Lynn stashed a $1350 bank draft, some Canadian cash, and $100 in American currency — more than most men made in a year. Also carrying a pile of letters written by homesick prospectors, clerks, and claims workers, and a marvellous nugget carried out for the Pavilion's new manager, Lynn was ready to hit the trail south.

A broken pedal on Fred Clayson's bicycle allowed Lynn to catch up to the cyclist, and the two men spent a companionable week's travel together. On Christmas Eve, they shared food and lodging with others at Captain John Fussell's roadhouse in the tiny riverfront settlement of Minto. Months later, people there remembered the moment the group gathered around Lynn to admire the golden curio he was carrying for his boss — a smaller nugget-within-a-nugget rattled around in a natural cavity of the larger piece. Nobody who saw it that day ever forgot it.

That same Christmas Eve, government telegraph lineman Lawrence "Ole" Olsen and a North-West Mounted Police constable were hitting the trail north, although not by choice. Somewhere out there, the telegraph line was down again. The newly installed communication link was a critical part of life in the Yukon. At no time in the year was the rapid *click-click-click* of the telegrapher's key more comforting than at Christmas. Happily, the men quickly located the problem, and the secured wire was singing with seasonal messages again. They, too, headed for Fussell's roadhouse, sharing the evening with Fred and Lynn.

Two other men were near the trail not far from Minto that fateful night and had something to celebrate, too — their freedom. George O'Brien and his new partner, "Little Tommy" Graves, had met inside the Dawson City lockup, where O'Brien was serving a year's sentence for theft. Released about the same time, the two former convicts had quickly put into play the plans O'Brien had formulated while sawing logs for the NWMP's hungry woodstoves.

George O'Brien had no desire to gasp and sweat underground simply to make a claim owner wealthy. Easier pickings were nestled cosily inside the packs travellers had strapped to their backs. O'Brien had a hunch that there would be plenty of travellers on the trail going out for the holiday. They had already met and talked with a few on their way out of Dawson.

On a secondary track not far from the main trail, the conniving pair built a snug little canvas-covered log quadrangle to call home. They stocked up with food stolen from an iced-in river scow and, accompanied by O'Brien's big yellow dog, settled in. All O'Brien and Graves had to do to make their Christmas merry and bright was wait and watch. Sooner or later, unsuspecting travellers would carry up the pair's "Christmas presents."

George O'Brien had planned it all very nicely. It was going to be a very merry Christmas.

The Search Begins

In Skagway, Will Clayson was having a frustrating Christmas Eve. Too bad Fred hadn't arrived. Oh well, maybe tomorrow,

Will must have thought as he called it a night, pulling up the blankets and blowing out the lamp.

Christmas Day crawled by. Waiting was worse than it ordinarily would have been, because it was the one day in the year Will didn't have the demands of storekeepers, traders, and packers to occupy his mind. Fred could have been delayed by any one of a dozen different problems. Rotten ice on one of the lakes. A stumble in deep snow. A simple sprain could mean death on the sub-zero trail. Will didn't want to think about it, but without work to keep him busy, that's where his mind wandered.

Days later — and still no sign of his brother — Will decided he couldn't wait and worry any longer. Leaving others in charge of the office and warehouse, he assembled his pack and booked the next train out of Skagway over the mountains to the closest NWMP post at Lake Bennett. His chances of finding Fred were slim, but it was better than sitting in Skagway fretting.

A week after Christmas, NWMP corporal Paddy Ryan halted his dog team in front of John Fussell's roadhouse. Ryan was a troubled man. He had invited Ole Olsen for Christmas dinner at his NWMP post in Hootchikoo, but Ole had never shown up. At first, Ryan had shrugged it off, figuring that the lineman must have been waylaid by another snapped telegraph line. However, his fears were raised when he learned that Ole had been at the roadhouse Christmas Eve, teaming up with travellers Lynn Relfe and Fred Clayson, and that all *three* should have been at the Hootchikoo Christmas dinner table.

When Ryan returned to his detachment, he had a surprise visit from Constable Frank Bacon. Bacon was in a foul mood. The telegraph line was out again and he was stumbling around in the snow trying to repair it himself. "Where's Olsen?" Ryan asked. "Nobody had seen Olsen for days," Bacon groused.

Ryan was on the trail early the next morning, running behind his dog team. The search for the missing men had begun.

Mushing his dog team down the main trail, Ryan spotted the opening to a smaller trail he had never explored that ran close to the bank of the frozen Yukon River. He decided to follow it. There, he came upon a small, canvas-roofed cabin. Moments later, after his eyes adjusted to the gloom inside the one-room structure, Ryan spied a tidy pile of boxes and sacks. Inside were tinned goods and biscuits, but it was what was stencilled on the outside that mattered most. The cartons were addressed to the MacKay Brothers, whose ice-bound scow had been found looted not long before.

Downriver at the NWMP post Fort Selkirk a few days later, Constable Alexander Pennycuick re-read Corporal Ryan's wire. For weeks, goaded by the MacKay brothers, Pennycuick had been hunting a pair who called themselves Miller and Ross. Pennycuick had actually met them once, in a short, tense campsite interaction. A nasty pair, the constable

140

thought. By the time he returned with an arrest warrant, the two had disappeared. Every Mountie on the river knew about the search. God bless Ryan — here was the break the constable had been waiting for!

On his way to Hootchikoo, Pennycuick searched the cabin Ryan had described in his telegram. A close examination of the stove revealed something he had noticed at Miller's camp: the unique pattern created by damper holes punched in the metal.

At Hootchikoo a few hours later, Pennycuick and Ryan compared notes and examined the 40-82 Winchester that Ryan had taken from the cabin. Why had the two left the rifle behind? Maybe they were in a hurry, desperate to get "outside," and simply forgot it. Understandably, Ryan seemed more concerned with the fate of Ole Olsen, but Pennycuick decided he had to move fast on Miller and Ross — he vowed he wouldn't lose them again.

Serious Questions

Every day, dozens of telegrams flashed back and forth between Yukon police detachments. Pennycuick added his own about Miller and Ross and a big, yellow-and-white Newfoundland dog. Hundreds of kilometres away, at Tagish, near Lake Bennett and White Pass, Staff Sergeant George Graham was soon to send a telegram of his own, about an ex-con named O'Brien.

One frigid afternoon, not long after Graham had

received the telegram from police in Dawson City asking officers to be on the lookout for Miller and Ross, the staff sergeant had found a pair of shivering, half-frozen horses outside the post's dog-puncher bunkhouse. The horses were still attached to a sleigh. Graham was shocked. Inside the sleigh lay an ice-stiffened NWMP buffalo robe. Now the staff sergeant was curious.

When Graham opened the bunkhouse door, he found a steaming George O'Brien and a big, panting dog standing next to the piping-hot wood stove. O'Brien's story? The sleigh had gone through the ice on the river — he was lucky to be alive. Graham couldn't blame any traveller for wanting to get warm, but in the Yukon, the welfare of horses came first. Now, what about that government-issue robe?

"I was on the woodpile last summer and when the police let me go they found that they had lost my robe. A good one it was, too," O'Brien explained nonchalantly. "So they gave me that one as a replacement."

Graham decided that, as soon as they got those horses rubbed down, he'd check out O'Brien's story with Dawson City.

In Dawson, somebody noticed Graham's telegram and remembered another wire had mentioned a similar dog. A quick check was all it took.

Two days later, George O'Brien, also known as Miller, was arrested in Tagish for cache theft. But who — and where — was "Ross?" At Hootchikoo, Corporal Paddy Ryan was still asking himself where Ole Olsen was, while downriver, the headlines in the *Dawson Daily News* asked readers "Where's Clayson?" and "Were They Murdered?"

Finding Answers

For Yukoners, murder committed in the heat of passion was a sad fact of life. However, if, indeed, the three men had been murdered, it was obviously no lover's crime of passion. It was likely murder for money. These were cold, calculated killings.

Goaded by the newspapers, the public demanded action. NWMP inspector William Scarth, a well-known and respected lawman, was put in charge of the case. However, as Scarth knew only too well, without bodies, nobody was sure that anyone had been murdered at all.

Back across the border in Skagway, after frustrating and fruitless visits with the Mounties, a desperate Will Clayson decided there was only one way to find out what happened to his brother — hire a professional detective. The man Will paid was stocky Philip Ralph Maguire, a former detective of the famed Pinkerton Agency, now working free-lance in Alaska. With the facts in his calculating mind, and Will's letter of introduction in his coat pocket, Maguire was off to Tagish to interview a certain NWMP prisoner.

At Tagish, George Graham quietly fumed. Somehow, when he examined all of O'Brien's belongings, he had failed to notice two $100 bills tucked beneath the leather sole of one of the prisoner's boot socks. Trust Philip Maguire to find them. Graham hated being shown up, especially by a civilian detective, an *American* civilian detective at that.

The staff sergeant shoved aside his personal bitterness and pondered the mystery like the professional he was. That was a lot of money for a jobless ex-con, he figured, especially when he considered that O'Brien still had that much money after buying a sleigh and two-horse team. Where had he found that money? Graham decided he would wire the others about that.

Maguire's next stop was Selkirk, where he and Paddy Ryan set out for O'Brien's little cabin. Once there, Maguire opened the stove and, a few moments later, held up his findings: three moccasin eyelets and a blackened metal buckle. Who used clothes for fuel in a wood stove?

A few days later, Maguire, Scarth, and Pennycuick met in Selkirk to discuss their woodstove findings. Ryan should have been at the meeting, too, but he had been called to attend to another urgent investigation. However, before he left, he scribbled a note for Maguire to take to Scarth, recommending that the inspector contract the American to help with the investigation. Scarth agreed and decided that Maguire and Pennycuick should return to the site of the cabin and continue to look for clues.

Outside the cabin, Maguire and Pennycuick studied the snow. Suddenly, near the sloping riverbank, the sled dogs went crazy, sniffing and yowling at the ground. Maguire dug into the snow and straightened up, staring down at a pool of frozen blood. Digging some more, he found a second frozen bloody pool.

"They burned the bodies," the private eye announced to the constable. Pennycuick shook his head. That was too much work. Instead, the policeman pointed to the river. "The bodies were shoved under the ice," he countered.

William Scarth arrived at the scene a few days later, as Maguire and Pennycuick continued their search for clues, something to firmly link O'Brien to the cabin site. That day, Pennycuick had decided to bring along O'Brien's dog. Seized with an idea, he suddenly bent down and uncoupled his leash.

"Go home!" he shouted to the animal. Obediently, the dog trotted toward the nearby tent-cabin. There, beneath a tree, the animal lay down in the snow. Pennycuick smiled at his open-mouthed companions. Scarth walked into the cabin while Maguire disappeared behind it. Within a few minutes, the American detective was back, showing the policemen an empty lime-juice bottle and old double-bit axe with three peculiar nicks in one blade. What other clues lay beneath the snow?

Clues to the Killings
Using small sticks, Maguire and Pennycuick painstakingly moved aside the top layers of snow near the tent-cabin. On benumbed hands and knees, eyes mere inches from the

snowy surface, they scoured the area around the cabin for other signs of murder.

They were not long in coming: eight other spots of blood, three empty 40-82 Winchester cartridges, bullet scarring on tree trunks, and a mashed bullet in one of the pools of blood. Maguire uncovered an unnerving find: a bone-and-tissue skull fragment. Pennycuick found a bit of paper snagged on a nearby willow. The words written on it had somehow survived the weather and read, quite clearly, "Monday, Dec 22nd 1899 Received L. Olson $6 for meals and bunk J. Fussell." Both investigators allowed themselves smiles of grim satisfaction. Poor Ole.

The list of discovered items grew: a crown from a molar, more burnt clothing, a pocket knife with a damaged blade, keys, a medicine bottle belonging to Olsen, and more cartridges from a 30-30 rifle and .41 calibre revolver, the type of weapons seized from O'Brien at Tagish. At Minto, John Fussell recognized the lime-juice bottle — he had filled one just like it with whisky and sold it to Ole Olsen.

After more than four months of active investigation, Ryan, Pennycuick, and Maguire had done all they could. Now, it was early May 1900. What the investigators needed more than anything else were bodies. Pennycuick was confident that Mother Nature would help them out. All they could do was wait.

They call it spring breakup. Since the first white prospector swirled a pan in a Yukon creek bed, men had awaited the warm temperatures that freed the ice from rivers and lakes. It meant easy travel, and lucky discoveries. In 1900, it meant the same thing to the NWMP, only the discoveries they made were gruesome rather than golden.

On May 30, a bullet-riddled body surfaced on a sand bar less than two kilometres from Fort Selkirk. A few days later, another body was discovered. Cards in a pocket read "Lynn Wallace Relfe." Like the first body, this one was torn by bullets, just how badly was revealed at the autopsy: Slugs had broken a rib, nicked the liver, burst the spleen, smashed the skull, and shattered the jaw. The crown of the third molar was missing. The crown found in the bush was deftly pressed into position on top of the damaged tooth — a perfect fit.

Near the end of June, a third body was found. There was no flesh left on the badly fractured skull, but Ole Olsen's prominent teeth were instantly recognizable to those who knew him. The charge against George O'Brien was now murder.

The Noose Tightens
Over 11 days of June 1901, inside Dawson City's old log courthouse, a parade of 63 witnesses gave testimony in what was, at that time, Canada's most expensive and notorious murder trial.

"The body of Relfe showed he had been shot in two places," Crown Prosecutor Fred Wade told the jury. "Clayson had been dealt with in much the same way, while with Olsen the method of procedure had been somewhat different, he being clubbed to death ... besides which, his head had been shot into an almost unrecognizable pulp." For those wedged into the overcrowded courtroom (and those outside straining at the windows for a peek), these were mere hints of what was to come.

One by one, the witnesses told their stories and explained the clues: How the police themselves had supplied O'Brien with the damaged axe that he used to cut trees down so he could spy on trail travellers; about the vent holes that identified O'Brien's stove; the dark stain on O'Brien's sleigh identified as blood. Yes, a saddened but satisfied Will Clayson testified — the keys (including ones that fit drawers in the Skagway office safe) and the pocket knife found near the cabin were his brother's.

Finally, there was O'Brien's former cellmate, Kid West, escorted north from Seattle's jail at great expense after he claimed O'Brien had asked him to be his partner in crime. However, those in the courtroom were stunned when similar testimony came, not from "a burglar, a thief, a gambler, a convicted criminal," as O'Brien's attorney scoffed, but from Chris Williams, an honest Dawson working man who claimed that O'Brien had offered him the same outrageous opportunity two years before. Williams' testimony was the one that mattered. Two hours later, the jury found George O'Brien guilty of murder.

Two months later, on his last day on earth, O'Brien's

composure slipped. Those standing outside the jail could hear him angrily shouting and cursing members of the police escort charged with leading him to the gallows. However, once on the scaffold, the murderer was curiously calm.

"Do you want to hear the truth?" he asked the sheriff as the noose was tightened around his neck. "I did not murder those men."

"Who did murder them, then?"

"I do not know, nor do I know anything about it."

The hangman pulled the hood over O'Brien's head and stepped back, and, a second later, George O'Brien's body was swaying beneath the floor.

* * *

Christmases came and went. Sometime during each holiday season, the men who investigated that long-ago triple Yuletide slaying likely paused and remembered their search for clues in the snow. The investigators — Maguire, Pennycuick, Ryan, and Scarth — must also have recalled another grisly discovery made long after the trial. When the decomposed, bullet-riddled body was found on the Yukon river bank, they must have wondered, What ever did become of O'Brien's partner in crime, Little Tommy Graves?

Bibliography

Adams, John. *Christmas in Old Victoria.* Victoria: Discover the Past, 2003.

Atkin, Ronald. *Maintain the Right: The Early History of the North West Mounted Police, 1873–1900.* London: MacMillan London Ltd., 1973.

Bronson, William. *The Last Grand Adventure.* New York: McGraw-Hill Book Company, 1977.

Coates, Ken S., and William R. Morrison. *Strange Things Done: Murder in Yukon History.* Montreal: McGill-Queens University Press, 2004.

Godspell, Philip. "Bloody Christmas" (typescript). Glenbow Archives, Calgary, n.d.

Kelly, Nora and William. *The Royal Canadian Mounted Police: A Century of History.* Edmonton: Hurtig Publishers, 1973.

Longstreth, T. Morris. *Murder at Belly Butte.* Toronto: The MacLean Publishing Co., 1931.

Malcolm, M. J. *Murder in the Yukon: The Case Against George O'Brien.* Saskatoon: Western Producer Prairie Books, 1982.

Chapter 9
The Greatest Gift of All

by Rich Mole

Pacing the pitching deck of the Hudson's Bay Company brigantine *Una,* Captain William Mitchell reflected on his promise to have the crew safely back from the Queen Charlotte Islands by Christmas. For the captain and his 20 hard-working mariners, home port was Fort Victoria, the company's fur-trading outpost on the southern tip of the Colony of Vancouver Island. The overly optimistic promise was "Auld Wullie's" brave attempt to mollify his men, already bitterly disappointed by the voyage's unexpected failure.

Mitchell's Christmas promise had been made confidently enough just a few days before. The *Una* had sailed out of the sheltered Queen Charlotte anchorage, at a place the men were now calling Mitchell Harbour, out of deference to the likable old salt.

Before long, however, a slow-building north Pacific storm had begun to lash the ship. Scanning the dark grey skies above the tossing sailing vessel on this Christmas Eve 1851, Mitchell now doubted his ability to make good on his Yuletide promise. He braced himself against the ship's wooden railing as another jet of stinging sea spray leaped high over the sharply angled deck. A fine Christmas this was turning out to be.

Just a few hours later, tying up at Fort Victoria in time to enjoy holiday merriment was the least of the captain's worries. He knew that if the storm did not abate or the ship failed to find shelter, there was a good chance none of them would ever arrive home.

A Voyage of Golden Opportunity

Weeks before, when they had made ready for the trip up the coast, every member of the crew had been excited, and with good reason. It wasn't every day that a man had a chance to be part of a treasure-hunting expedition. And the treasure the *Una* was being sent to find was gold.

The profit-hungry HBC didn't send its ships off on mere speculation. A few months before, at the north coast post of Fort Simpson, Hudson's Bay Company chief trader W. H. McNeill had received samples of gold-bearing quartz from friendly Queen Charlotte Island Native people. The visitors actually offered to sell the HBC their land, all but begging the company men to come and dig for the gold. They knew the presence of the heavy, yellow-and-white rocks seemed the best enticement to persuade the company men to visit the islands and protect them from warlike rival Haida chiefs.

McNeill guessed that the real intention of his visitors was the protection the HBC men would offer and wasn't particularly impressed with the ore samples anyway. However, he dutifully sent them down to Fort Victoria, where they certainly impressed others. Chief Factor James Douglas ordered Captain William Mitchell to take the *Una* out on a summertime voyage of investigation. While the ship's company found nothing of value, the Native peoples there had offered to sell what they had unearthed earlier. These additional samples were enough to convince the company to send Mitchell out again, in early October.

Unlike the *Una*'s first trip, this was to be no brief survey of the beach. The HBC had underwritten a major six-month mining expedition that would take members of the crew farther inland to search out gold-bearing rock. The company ensured the crew had a stake in the journey's outcome by offering each man a share of the gold in lieu of wages.

As events had recently demonstrated farther south, gold fever was a particularly contagious malady, infecting men thousands of kilometres from prospectors' discoveries. Just four years before, the enormously rich gold find at Sutter's Mill in Spanish California had prompted a continental migration of gigantic proportions. The Mexican-held territory had become an American state just a few months before the gold discovery on the northern island.

Now, with the California gold rush already a memory, speculation ran wild. Where was the next big strike likely to take place? Some HBC officers were betting that it would be on the Queen Charlotte Islands.

About the time the *Una* was casting off at the HBC dock on its second voyage, a former HBC employee informed the *Oregon Spectator* that the company had found "specimens of virgin gold and gold bearing quartz ... the latter of the richest quality that [he] ever saw." The news was out.

James Douglas realized that the most immediate threat would be the loss of mineral wealth in the company's own territory. American vessels would, he wrote, "carry the product of the mines into their own ports in Oregon and California to the manifest injury of Her Majesty's possessions in these quarters." However, there was much more than mere gold at stake.

Douglas knew only too well how high the cost of lack of foresight and control could be. Mexico had lost California. The Hudson's Bay Company had lost Oregon and Washington territories. The newly commissioned colonial governor could imagine the Americans taking over the entire north coast. So when Douglas dispatched the *Una* in early October 1851, he did so as a symbol of the HBC's ownership of the north coast. He did not expect to see the ship again until March 1852.

The Fight for Riches

Now, months before her anticipated spring departure, the *Una* was entering the Strait of Juan de Fuca on the last tempestuous leg of her return home. In her hold was just a tiny fraction of the gold the men had hoped to bring out. What made their hasty departure all the more frustrating was that Mitchell, his crew, and the expedition leader, W. H. McNeill, were certain there was much more gold than previously suspected.

Given the investment deal they had made with the company, it was easy for the men to feel the voyage was a failure. Realizing the area's great potential, Mitchell and McNeill shared the crew's feelings. The vein of gold that was worked by the group measured 15 to 18 centimetres wide and extended some 15 metres down the beach before angling into the bush. One member of the crew managed to pry more than 30 grams of pure gold out of the ground within half an hour, using nothing more than a chisel.

A day or two on the island was all it took to make the once-dubious McNeill a believer. "The rock proved to be rich in gold," he wrote in his report. "In my opinion, gold will be found in many places hereafter, in the west side of the island."

Careful use of dynamite revealed an even more exciting discovery below the surface. The 21 kilograms of ore stored in the ship's large strongbox was rich enough to yield more than 2 kilograms of pure gold, "a rate of return," Chief Factor

Douglas later confided, that would "make a very great profit in the course of a few months' work."

However, the men of the *Una* had also not expected to encounter the aggressive competition they did once the wealth hidden below the ground was blasted onto the surface. As soon as the smoke cleared from each explosion, it became a vicious race between members of the Haida tribe and the *Una*'s vastly outnumbered crewmen for possession of the newly revealed riches. As the sailors attempted to gather the shattered gold-bearing rock, the Haida men bullied and badgered them for every valuable chunk of ore.

Pushing, shoving, and shouting matches raged between the island's people — who insisted vehemently that the land, and the gold it held, was theirs — and the gold-hungry crew, who knew that each lost piece of rock represented a loss in pay. The Haida people drew their knives and confiscated the crew's tools as well.

Tension increased and, with it, the likelihood that belligerence would accelerate into bloodshed. The lure of gold had far greater power over the young Haida men than their elders. In desperation, the Haida chiefs implored expedition leaders to leave the area. Angry, sullen crewmen were ordered back to the ship. To avoid the bloodshed he was sure would follow, Mitchell sailed the *Una* out of the harbour less than three weeks after it had first dropped anchor.

If the trip had proceeded as planned, the *Una* would have remained safely snugged in the island's sheltering cove for the duration of the winter. But her premature departure forced her out onto the open ocean, vulnerable to quickly changing winter weather conditions. Mitchell's worst fear had come true: a sudden winter storm quickly bore down on his ship.

At first, the captain determined that the safest course of action was to keep clear of the coastline. The primitive charts he squinted over held out one hope, indicating that he might take shelter in Neah Bay, on Cape Flattery. The fact that the destination was in American territory was of little consequence. Once in the bay, Mitchell hoped that the *Una* could simply wait out the weather.

Tomorrow, alas, there would be no Christmas dinner in the Fort Victoria mess hall for captain and crew. There would be no steaming platters of grouse and venison, no tankards of port and brandy to share with friends and colleagues. At least, the captain consoled himself, they would all be alive to see the new year.

A Jinxed Ship and a Threatened Crew

As the ship entered Neah Bay, horrified crewmen heard a low, rumbling counterpoint to the high-pitched wail of the wind. What their ears had caught was the ominous sound every sailor dreads: the grinding of wood against rock, quickly followed by the agonized shriek of splintering hull timbers. The *Una* shuddered sickeningly to a halt.

When members of the crew picked themselves up from

the listing deck, they needed no one to tell them what had happened: the ship had run aground on a hidden reef. Those below clambered up onto the deck to report that the *Una* was rapidly taking on water.

Mitchell quickly deduced that it was already too late to save the ship. Saving lives and the ship's precious cargo became his priorities. He ordered them all into the boats with everything that they could manhandle off the ship, including furs loaded from Fort Simpson and the gold they had managed to carry aboard from Mitchell Harbour.

The ship's predicament had caught the attention of sailors aboard the American vessel *Susanna*, which was lying at anchor nearby. But others were also watching the *Una's* plight with more than casual interest. On shore just a short distance away, members of the Makah tribe sat at their campfires near the fringe of dense rainforest, watching the first boats pull away from the settling ship. The Makahs moved quickly, gathering near their canoes at the water's edge.

Those hauling the first of the *Una's* boats up on the rocky beach thought the Native people launching their canoes were preparing to help their shipmates escape the foundering vessel. It's unlikely any of them knew the history of these people they were greeting with outstretched hands and grateful smiles. Scarcely five years earlier, the Makahs had attacked a Clallum settlement and, for a time, lay siege to the fortified outpost. Here, now, a stranded vessel provided another opportunity for plunder.

As the sailors began to wrestle their large, heavy sea-men's chests out of the boats, other hands were soon at work. But when crewmen went to thank the Native people who were assisting them, they were abruptly shoved away from their cargo. The startled crewmen pushed back. Then the Makahs started to open the chests. Shouting in protest, the unarmed crewmen began to grapple with the thieves. As the stumbling men wrestled with one another in the loose gravel, other Makah men began to deftly slide their canoes into the water.

The shouts of the men on the beach quickly alerted those remaining on board the *Una*. As alarmed as Mitchell was by the violently struggling figures on shore, it was the line of rapidly approaching canoes that concerned him most. The rascals were about to board and pillage his ship! The crew redoubled its efforts to offload the furs and gold.

Within minutes, the first of the Makah men had climbed over the ship's side, and the handful of crew left aboard engaged in a series of frenzied, man-to-man struggles. Punching, pushing, and gouging, the men fought on in an attempt to buy the captain and other shipmates a few precious moments to launch the last boats. In the melee that followed, men even lost their clothing as coats, shoes, and shirts were wrenched and ripped from their bodies by the boarders.

Meanwhile, swinging their oars, the men on the beach fought off their attackers and somehow cleared the shoreline without leaving a single soul behind. Together, these blood-ied combatants from the beach and the deck of the *Una* made their way toward the *Susanna* as fast as they could.

A few minutes later, helping hands lifted Mitchell and his men on board. The captain took some solace in the fact that he and the others had managed to salvage the furs and the gold. However, the *Una*'s fate was a different matter. American and British sailors alike stood in stunned silence, watching the racing figures on the HBC brigantine. The sounds of looting and destruction carried across the bay's calm waters.

Una's Fiery Christmas

In all the chaos and confusion, another American vessel, the *Susan Sturgis,* commanded by Captain Matthew Rooney, had quietly entered the bay. The *Susanna* had no plans to move on immediately, but the *Susan Sturgis* did, so Rooney offered to transfer the *Una*'s men back home.

Although he accepted the humanitarian gesture with good grace, Mitchell undoubtedly recognized the bitter irony of the situation, for the destination of the American ship was the Queen Charlotte Islands and its quest identical to that of the HBC brigantine — the *Susan Sturgis* had been commis-sioned to seek out the gold that the men of the *Una* had been so forcefully denied.

By nightfall, while Rooney's crew made the HBC men as comfortable as they could, all three captains gathered for an unorthodox Christmas Eve get-together. This was no sociable celebration of the season, but a strategic planning conference. At stake was HBC property, and perhaps the very lives of its employees.

Could the *Una* be salvaged? Perhaps. She lay in fairly shallow water and was in no danger of sinking entirely. Might she actually be pulled off the rock? Possibly, the captains agreed. While there were still Makah men on board, many had fled to shore with the arrival of the *Susan Sturgis*. With the combined crews of three ships, retaking the *Una* would not be too difficult.

The more unpredictable factor was the winter weather. All the hard work undertaken to repair the vessel would be for naught if the weather changed. Stuck fast, the *Una* was as vulnerable as ever. Another storm might destroy her completely before repairs were finished and any refloating manoeuvres completed.

But then a more practical question was posed: was the *Una* worth salvaging? As the hours progressed, there appeared to be less and less worth salvaging. The crew watched the Makahs haul down the sails, carry off the rigging, and toss overboard provisions, storage containers, furniture, and anything else that wasn't nailed down.

Soon enough, the intruders had made Mitchell's decision for him.

Later that night, he was called up onto the deck of the *Susan Sturgis*. What he saw then he hoped he would never see again. The night sky was ominously alight. The proud HBC trading vessel was aflame along most of her length. For close to an hour, the fire roared and snapped, eating away at the ship before the disbelieving eyes of rescued and rescuers alike.

Was the fire an accident (the Makahs had carried on their destructive operation by torchlight), or was the ship deliberately set ablaze? Such speculation was, at that point, purely academic. In the dismal light of early morning — Christmas morning — nothing much remained of the *Una*. The ship had burned to the waterline.

A Not-So-Happy New Year

In the days following Christmas, the *Susan Sturgis* anchored below the palisades of Fort Victoria, and the *Una's* men were rowed ashore to family and friends. As the doomed brigantine's story passed from person to person around Fort Victoria's bastions, stores, and mess hall, there was much cause for celebration. The men were back! Given the outrageous misfortunes and dangers they had endured, perhaps they had received the most precious of all Christmas gifts: their lives.

In fact, despite the disappointment of their failed treasure hunt, the *Una's* men actually had the happiest new year of all who sought Queen Charlotte gold. The ill-fated trip of an American vessel ended when winter winds set the ship adrift from her Queen Charlotte anchorage. When the desperate crew finally staggered out of the surf, they were set upon by Haida. Worth more alive than dead, the men were held for weeks until the captain of another American ship managed to purchase their freedom.

Months after, Chief Trader McNeill watched five near-naked men stumble out of Haida canoes at the end of the Fort Simpson wharf. As the shivering men stood nearby, McNeill bartered successfully for their release. One of the group gratefully introduced himself as Captain Matthew Rooney of the *Susan Sturgis*. The vessel, her captain, and her crew of seven had met the same fate as those aboard the *Una*, when Graham Island warriors plundered the vessel and set her afire.

Down at Fort Victoria, these reports of life-threatening but fruitless searches for gold must have had William Mitchell shaking his head in sad disbelief. After the *Una*'s fiery demise, Douglas had sent Mitchell out again to the Queen Charlottes, this time with a large complement of 40 men. The chief trader on board summed up the results of this last HBC gold exploration in two words: "very unproductive." It seemed that the rich vein of gold that paralleled the beach in Mitchell Harbour was what prospectors called "a blow" — a misleading freak of geology. All gold-bearing quartz soon petered away to nothing.

Regardless, Christmas 1852 was an occasion for both thanksgiving and celebration at Fort Victoria. Inside the mess hall, it was a merry affair, with fiddling, dancing, singing, and feasting.

Holiday Misadventures

As he played host to it all, Governor James Douglas was likely in a suitably celebratory mood. All those in the company's employ had returned from the Queen Charlottes to Fort Victoria in safety that year. And while the islands' golden riches remained a wistful dream, one more important dream had become a reality — Douglas was now lieutenant-governor of the Queen Charlotte Islands and their proud peoples. In the decades to come, the islands themselves were to prove a much more enduring gift than their elusive gold.

Bibliography

Adams, John. *Christmas in Old Victoria.* Victoria: Discover the Past, 2003.

Bosfield, Hartwell. *Fort Victoria Letters.* Winnipeg: Hudson's Bay Record Society, 1979.

Dalzell, Kathleen. *The Queen Charlotte Islands Vol. 1: 1774–1966.* Queen Charlotte City, BC: Bill Ellis Books, 1968.

Douglas, James. "Letters Outward, Jan.-Feb., 1852." British Columbia Archives, Victoria.

Haynes, Bessie Doak. "Gold on Queen Charlotte's Island," *The Beaver,* Winter 1966.

McKelvie, B. A. "The Wreck of the Una." *Vancouver Daily Province,*

December 24, 1949.

Nesbitt, James. "Salty Old Sailor." *Daily Colonist,* April 4, 1963.

"Saga of the Brigantine Una" (typescript). British Columbia Archives, Victoria, n.d.

About the Authors

Johanna Bertin has long been fascinated with Sable Island, and researching the story of the *Frances* was a labour of love. Johanna has written three other books for Altitude Publishing: *Strange Events: Incredible Canadian Monsters, Curses, Ghosts, and Other Tales; Strange Events and More: Canadian Giants, Witches, Wizards, and Other Tales;* and *Sable Island: Tales of Tragedy and Survival from the Graveyard of the Atlantic.* She is working on her next book, *Strange Events of the East Coast.* Johanna lives in Smithfield, NB.

Joyce Glasner studied gold and silversmithing at the New Brunswick School of Craft and Design before earning her BA with honours in English at Saint Mary's University in Halifax. She is an editor, freelance writer, and the author of *The Halifax Explosion: Surviving the Blast that Shook a Nation; Christmas in Atlantic Canada: Heartwarming Legends, Tales, and Traditions;* and *Pirates and Privateers: Swashbuckling Stories from the East Coast.* Joyce lives in Halifax, NS.

Andrew Hind is a freelance writer whose feature articles have appeared in magazines and newspapers in Canada, the United States, and England. He developed a passion for history early on, especially for unusual and obscure events and